15
MINUTE
MEALS

Photography by *"Lord" David Loftus*
Design by *Interstate Associates*
Cover by *Superfantastic*

15
MINUTE
MEALS

HarperCollins*Publishers*Ltd

TO MY WONDERFUL WIFE,
JOOLS, AND OUR FOUR
GORGEOUS, SWEET AND
LOVING LITTLE MONSTERS
— POPPY, DAISY, PETAL AND
BUDDY. LOVE YOU. DAD XX

My babys

15-Minute Meals

Copyright © 2012 by Jamie Oliver. All rights reserved.
Photography © 2012 by Jamie Oliver Enterprises Limited.
All rights reserved.
Photography: David Loftus

Published by HarperCollins Publishers Ltd

First published in the United Kingdom in 2012 by Penguin Books Ltd.
First published in Canada by HarperCollins Publishers Ltd in this
hardcover edition: 2013

No part of this book may be used or reproduced in any manner
whatsoever without the prior written permission of the publisher,
except in the case of brief quotations embodied in reviews.

HarperCollins books may be purchased for educational, business,
or sales promotional use through our Special Markets Department.

HarperCollins Publishers Ltd
2 Bloor Street East, 20th Floor
Toronto, Ontario, Canada
M4W 1A8

www.harpercollins.ca

Library and Archives Canada Cataloguing in Publication
information is available upon request.

ISBN 978-1-44342-925-2

Printed in Italy by Graphicom
Color reproduction by Altaimage Ltd

9 8 7 6 5 4 3 2 1

www.jamieoliver.com

SIMPLE

I'M SO EXCITED THAT YOU'RE STEPPING INTO THE WORLD OF *15-MINUTE MEALS*. THE PROMISE OF THIS BOOK IS SIMPLE: DELICIOUS, NUTRITIOUS, SUPER-FAST FOOD THAT'S A TOTAL JOY TO EAT AND PERFECT FOR BUSY PEOPLE LIKE YOU AND ME.

MY RELATIONSHIP WITH YOU, THE PUBLIC, AND THESE COOKBOOKS I WRITE IS AN INCREDIBLY IMPORTANT ONE. OVER 30 MILLION OF YOU HAVE BOUGHT MY BOOKS IN THE LAST 10 YEARS, AND I NEVER TAKE THAT AMAZING SUPPORT FOR GRANTED. WITH EACH NEW BOOK I FEEL A MASSIVE RESPONSIBILITY TO PUSH MYSELF AND GIVE YOU SOMETHING I REALLY BELIEVE IN; SOMETHING I THINK YOU WILL LOVE, WITH RECIPES THAT DELIVER ON EVERY LEVEL, AND THIS BOOK IS NO EXCEPTION. IT'S HAD A CLEAR GAME PLAN RIGHT FROM THE START, BECAUSE NOT ONLY AM I RESPONDING TO WHAT YOU ARE ALL SCREAMING OUT FOR – TASTY, QUICK, AFFORDABLE FOOD – I'M DOING IT WITH RECIPES THAT ARE ANCHORED IN BALANCE AND NUTRITION. **THE CREATION OF THIS BOOK HAS BEEN A REAL GAME CHANGER FOR ME.**

There are a lot of days when speed is key, and that's where *15-Minute Meals* comes into play. This book is categorically a tool to make you cook really fast, delicious, fresh food, any day of the week. Of course, slow cooking old-school, authentic recipes is the heart and soul of any great home cook, but this book is an expression of big, exciting flavors, fast, for busy people.

Developing and writing the recipes, designing the pages, getting the timings right, and bringing the calories and nutrition to this happy place without compromising on flavor has all taken an awful lot of hard work. Every word, every sentence, has been debated, and every single stage of each recipe has been streamlined in order to give you these super-quick, tasty dishes. I can't tell you how hard it's been. I've had to be ruthless, rein myself in, and carefully weigh up every decision I've made, from the amount of ingredients I've used to the number of pans on the stove. But it's been totally worth it, because my food team and I are so excited about where we've finally got to with this book. So please trust in all the effort we've put in, and know that as long as you follow what I've written, and have the essential equipment that is vital for speed, you'll be enjoying these tasty, healthy meals in your own home, possibly even tonight.

NUTRITIOUS
TOTAL JOY TO EAT

Because I passionately wanted this to be a cookbook you can use every day of the week, and not just for special occasions, health and nutrition had to be at the heart of it. So I wrote and cooked every recipe with my incredible nutritionists, Laura Parr and her team, looking over my shoulder. They kept me on track, and kept a close eye on portion size, and as a result the recipes in this book are averaging about 580 calories per serving, which is great, so they'll fit easily into any main meal based on what we should be eating each day. It's really important to vary your recipe choices so that you feed your body with lots of different nutrients. Most importantly – because calories can be a useful but slightly blunt measure – keep in mind that these tasty meals are packed full of whole foods, grains, veggies, fresh herbs, citrus, quality proteins and other beautiful things that will really help take care of you and your family.

I've taken inspiration from all over the world for these dishes, and they are undeniably delicious. But for me, the best thing of all is the fact that great flavors, unbelievable speed and nutritious, proper, everyday food can now come together in the same package.

Ultimately, *15-Minute Meals* is a frame of mind, and I think if you give it a go you'll really get into it. It's fun, dynamic, no-nonsense cooking. Yes, the first couple of times you cook a recipe it might take a little longer, but that's OK, it's not a race. There's a rhythm to these lovely recipes, and each has its own kind of beat. Once you embrace that and get into the spirit of the shortcuts and tips that I've given you, you'll definitely start knocking these meals out of the park in 15 minutes. And of course, it's not just about me as a chef being able to do it. These recipes have also been tested by cooks at all levels, from teenagers and seniors to busy mums and dads, and their response has mirrored the excitement that my team and I have – so positive and enthusiastic. Every one of them has helped me navigate the recipes into the shape they're in today. If they can do it, so can you.

FAST

The food in this book is tasty, it's got attitude, and it's just as at home being served to a house full of students as it is by parents to their children.

I know there's a perception out there that real food costs much more to cook than fast food does, but that's a fallacy; the average cost of a tasty balanced meal in this book is about $5.90 per person – and that's using lovely, quality ingredients – which the majority of the time is way cheaper than an equivalent pre-packaged meal, takeout or bucket of junk food. And if you get your weekly shopping routine down, and get your head and cooking skills in the *15-Minute Meals* zone, it's even quicker than going out to pick up dinner from a drive-through. Of course pre-prepared food can have a useful place in your diet once in a while; I just passionately believe that this book can help empower and encourage people of all ages to want to make real food for themselves more often than not.

DELICIOUS

SO THERE YOU GO, GUYS – THAT'S THE *15-MINUTE MEAL* PHILOSOPHY: FAST, TASTY, AFFORDABLE, GOOD-FOR-YOU FOOD. I GENUINELY HOPE YOU EMBRACE IT, BECAUSE I'M BUZZING ABOUT THIS IN SO MANY WAYS. IT'S ALL HERE FOR YOU, SO TAKE THE PHILOSOPHY ON BOARD AND RUN WITH IT. GOOD LUCK – I KNOW YOU CAN DO IT.

15

IMPORTANT
HOW TO SERVE

Investing in a handful of large platters, boards and bowls is absolutely essential to the essence of *15-Minute Meals* – this is about family-service, sharing and getting amongst it. Ultimately the food is going to taste great whatever you serve it on, but if you're dishing up on random, average plates, you're totally missing the point. It doesn't have to be expensive – make your own boards with food-safe paint, like I do, or go to flea markets and pick up platters and bowls. Happy hunting.

VERY IMPORTANT
HOW TO COOK FAST

If you want to cook these tasty meals in 15 minutes, you must have these kitchen gadgets, utensils and bits of equipment. If you don't, you simply won't get the meals done in time. This is not a complex list, and to be frank, you can pick it all up super-cheap these days if you want to (feel free to spend a bit more if you've got it). A food processor, blender, immersion blender and kettle are an absolute must – no compromise – they're essential. Good luck.

Equipment List

	Pestle & mortar
A good food processor	Garlic press
Blender	Tongs
Immersion blender	Slotted spatula
Microwave	Wooden spoons
Kettle	Slotted spoon
	Spatula
Grill pan	Potato masher
Ovenproof frying pans	Vegetable peeler
(roughly 12 in/10 in/8 in)	
Lidded pans	Box grater
(roughly 10 in/8 in/6 in)	Fine grater
2-level bamboo steamer	
Large sturdy high-sided	Measuring cups
roasting pans	Measuring spoons
Large non-stick baking pans	Scales
	Can opener
3 good-quality knives	Rolling pin
(chef's/paring/bread)	Bottle opener
Plastic cutting board	
Wooden cutting boards	Large serving
	platters, boards,
Mixing bowls	& bowls
Colander	
Sieve/strainer	

HOW TO OWN YOUR KITCHEN

I've seen a lot of kitchens in my time, and bad organization is phenomenally common. It will hold you back in your cooking, so simply clear out the clutter and the random stuff like piggy banks and magazines that gather on surfaces but have nothing to do with food. It's common sense really: anything used for prep or stirring should be near to where you cook – everything around that area should be the kit you use most frequently, whether it's storage, knives, pans, even the fridge. This will allow you to be instinctive and fast in the kitchen. Happy spring clean.

Pantry List

Baking: all-purpose flour, cocoa powder, cornstarch, desiccated coconut, dried apricots, light brown sugar, old-fashioned rolled oats, rose water, self-rising flour, vanilla paste or extract

Dried herbs & spices: Cajun seasoning, caraway seeds, cayenne pepper, Chinese five-spice powder, cinnamon sticks, cumin seeds, curry leaves, dill, dried red chiles, dry mustard powder, fennel seeds, fenugreek seeds, garam masala, ground allspice, ground cinnamon, ground cloves, ground coriander, ground ginger, kaffir lime leaves, mustard seeds, nutmeg, oregano, saffron, smoked chipotle or ancho chiles, smoked paprika, sweet smoked paprika, thyme, turmeric

Dried pasta & noodles: egg noodles, farfalle, fettuccine, fusilli, linguine, macaroni, orecchiette, penne, shells, spaghetti, whole-wheat fusilli & spaghetti, thin rice noodles

Jams & spreads: blackberry jam, cranberry jam, honey, peanut butter

Jarred food: grated horseradish, passata, preserved lemons, roasted red peppers, sun-dried tomatoes

Mustards: Dijon, English, grainy

Nuts & seeds (unsalted): blanched almonds, blanched hazelnuts, blanched peanuts, pine nuts, raw cashews, raw pistachios, raw pumpkin seeds, raw sesame seeds, raw sunflower seeds, raw walnut halves, whole Brazil nuts,

Oils: canola, extra virgin olive, olive, sesame, truffle

Pastes: harissa, miso paste or powder, Patak's curry pastes (korma, rogan josh, tikka), sun-dried tomato tapenade, tomato paste

Pickled & jarred vegetables: cauliflower, cornichons, gherkins, ginger, jalapeño chiles, red cabbage

Rice, grains & pulses: basmati rice, bulgur, couscous, fine cornmeal, quinoa, Uncle Ben's 10-minute wholegrain brown rice, Uncle Ben's ready-made wholegrain brown or basmati rice

Sauces: black bean, hoisin, hot chili, HP, low-salt soy, mint, quality mayonnaise, sweet chili, Tabasco, Teriyaki, tomato ketchup, Worcestershire

Tinned foods: anchovy fillets, chickpeas, diced tomatoes, light coconut milk, mixed beans, pineapple chunks, red kidney beans, red split lentils, water chestnuts

Vinegars: balsamic, red wine, rice or white, sherry

Miscellaneous: chicken & vegetable bouillon cubes, green tea bags

YOUR PANTRY

Here's my shopping list for a well-stocked pantry. These ingredients are really good flavor investments, and they pop up throughout the book. I love the fact that once you've stocked your shelves they're just ready, waiting for you to cook, so that they can brighten up your food. And they're nearly all non-perishable. If you want, go to *www.jamieoliver.com/15pantrylist* and you can get this list in an easy format that you can print out or view online, so that you can checklist what you need for next time you're shopping.

When it comes to fresh ingredients, if it's within your means, I strongly recommend supporting higher welfare and sustainable options for eggs, meat, fish, mayo, bouillon cubes, egg noodles and pasta. In return, this mindfulness will nearly always give you better flavor and will make you feel better about your impact on the world.

CHICKEN

CHICKEN DIM SUM
COCONUT BUNS, CUCUMBER PICKLE & HOISIN SAUCE

SERVES 4 | 795 CALORIES

Ingredients out • Kettle boiled • Food processor (metal blade)
• 16 large cupcake paper liners • Two 10-inch bamboo steamers
• Wok, medium-high heat • Small frying pan, low heat

Coconut buns

1 x 14-oz can of light coconut milk

2 coconut milk cans (1 lb)
self-rising flour, plus extra
for dusting

Chicken, pickles & garnishes

2 x 7-oz skinless boneless chicken
breasts

5 oz mixed mushrooms

3 tbsp hoisin sauce, plus
extra to serve

2 limes

1 bunch of broccolini

1 English cucumber

1 tbsp reduced-sodium soy sauce

1 tbsp rice or white wine vinegar

½ bunch of fresh cilantro

3 tbsp raw sesame seeds

3 tbsp pickled ginger

1–2 fresh red chiles

START COOKING

Pour the coconut milk into the processor with 2 heaping cans' worth of self-rising flour, whiz to a dough, then tip onto a flour-dusted worktop • Roll the dough into a sausage shape, cut into 8 even-sized pieces, then place each one into a double-layered paper liner, and squeeze those into one layer of the steamer • Pour 2 inches of boiling water into the wok, put the basket of buns on top with the lid on and leave to steam hard

Cut the chicken into ½-inch strips and toss in a bowl with the roughly torn mushrooms, hoisin sauce, juice of ½ a lime and a pinch of salt • Tip into the second steamer basket along with the trimmed broccolini and pop underneath the tray of buns for 5 minutes until cooked through • Peel the cucumber into ribbons, toss in a bowl with the soy sauce, vinegar and a few torn cilantro leaves, then with clean hands squeeze and scrunch everything together to make a pickle

Toast the sesame seeds in the frying pan until golden, then tip into a little bowl, cut the remaining 1½ limes into wedges, and serve with the pickled ginger and extra hoisin sauce in little bowls • Serve the buns and chicken in the steamer trays, scattering everything with the remaining cilantro leaves and finely sliced chile

CHICKEN TIKKA
LENTIL, SPINACH & NAAN SALAD

SERVES 4 | 607 CALORIES

Ingredients out • Grill pan, high heat
• Small frying pan, medium-low heat • Blender

Chicken

2 x 7-oz skinless boneless chicken
    breasts
2 heaping tsp Patak's tikka
    (medium) curry paste
4 cremini mushrooms

Salad

4 scallions
1 fresh red chile
1 heaping tsp mustard seeds
½ tsp cumin seeds
olive oil
½ x 19-oz can of lentils (drained
    and rinsed)
1 ripe tomato
red wine vinegar
1 big bunch of fresh cilantro
2 lemons
¼ cup fat-free plain yogurt
1 heaping tbsp unsalted raw
    cashew nuts
1 heaping tbsp mango chutney
1 tsp turmeric
2 naan breads, or other flatbreads
4 large handfuls baby spinach
½ English cucumber
1 carrot
1 oz feta cheese

START COOKING

On a large sheet of parchment paper, toss the chicken with salt, pepper and the tikka paste • Fold over the paper, then bash and flatten the chicken to ¾-inch thick with a rolling pin • Place on the hot grill pan with the halved mushrooms, turning after 3 or 4 minutes, until nicely charred and cooked through • Trim and finely slice the scallions and half the chile

Put the mustard and cumin seeds and 2 tablespoons of oil into the frying pan, followed by the sliced scallions and chile • Tip the lentils into the pan, squash in the tomato and add a pinch of salt and pepper and a splash of red wine vinegar • Toss occasionally for a couple of minutes, then turn the heat off • Rip the cilantro stalks into the blender with the juice of 1 lemon, the yogurt, cashews, mango chutney and turmeric, then whiz up until smooth

Remove the cooked chicken and mushrooms from the grill pan and put the naan on the pan • Tip the baby spinach onto a serving board or platter, scatter over the lentils, peel the cucumber and carrot over the top and sprinkle over the mushrooms • Slice the chicken, naan and remaining chile and arrange on top, then crumble over the feta and spoon over the dressing • Finish with the cilantro leaves and serve with lemon wedges

SPICY CAJUN CHICKEN
SMASHED SWEET POTATO & FRESH CORN SALSA

SERVES 4 | 651 CALORIES

Ingredients out • *Kettle boiled* • *Grill pan, high heat* • *Food processor (fine slicer)*
• *Large lidded saucepan, high heat* • *Large frying pan, medium-high heat*

Salsa
4 corn cobs (husks removed)
1 small bunch of fresh cilantro
1 fresh red chile
4 scallions
3 ripe tomatoes
2 limes
1 tbsp extra virgin olive oil

Smash
1 ½ lbs sweet potatoes
2 tbsp sweet red chili sauce

Chicken
4 x 4-oz skinless boneless chicken
   breasts
1 tbsp Cajun seasoning
1 tbsp fine ground cornmeal
olive oil
2 rashers of smoked bacon
6 oz okra
¾ oz feta cheese

START COOKING

Put the corn on the grill pan, turning when charred • Wash the sweet potatoes, remove any gnarly bits of skin with a vegetable peeler, then finely slice in the processor • Put the sweet potatoes into the large saucepan, then just cover with boiling salted water and the lid • On a large sheet of parchment paper, toss the chicken with salt, the Cajun seasoning and cornmeal • Fold over the paper, then bash and flatten the chicken to ¾-inch thick with a rolling pin

Put the chicken into the frying pan with 2 tablespoons of olive oil, turning after 3 or 4 minutes, until golden and cooked through • Drain the cooked sweet potatoes well, return to the pan and mash with the sweet chili sauce, pop the lid on and leave on a very low heat • Slice the bacon and add to the frying pan • As soon as the bacon starts to crisp up, add the okra to the pan

Carefully hold the charred corn steady and run a knife down the sides to cut off the kernels, then put them into a bowl • Roughly chop the top leafy half of the cilantro and add to the corn • Finely slice the chile and trimmed scallions, chop the tomatoes, and add to the bowl with a pinch of salt, the lime juice and extra virgin olive oil, then mix well • Serve the sweet potato smash on a board or platter with the chicken and okra, crumble over the feta, and serve with the fresh salsa on the side

INCREDIBLY DELICIOUS
CHICKEN SALAD

SERVES 4 | 557 CALORIES

Ingredients out • Kettle boiled • Medium lidded saucepan, high heat • Frying pan, high heat • Grill pan, high heat

Salad

1 head of broccoli

4 x 4-oz skinless boneless chicken breasts

1 heaping tsp ground coriander

olive oil

1 mug (10 oz) of bulgur

2 preserved lemons

1 bunch of radishes

2 scallions

½ bunch of fresh mint

2 tbsp extra virgin olive oil

3 tbsp red wine vinegar

2 tbsp unsalted raw sunflower seeds

1 cup sprouted cress

To serve

¼ cup fat-free plain yogurt

2 tsp harissa

1 lemon

START COOKING

Fill the medium saucepan with boiling salted water • Trim the end off the broccoli stalk, then cut up the broccoli head and add to the pan, cover and boil for 4 minutes • On a large sheet of parchment paper, toss the chicken with salt, pepper and the ground coriander, then fold the paper over and bash and flatten to ¾-inch thick with a rolling pin • Put into the frying pan with 2 tablespoons of olive oil, turning after 3 or 4 minutes, until golden and cooked through

With tongs, remove and drain the broccoli (leaving the pan of water on the heat), then place on the grill until nicely charred • Add 1 mug of bulgur and the preserved lemons to the broccoli water and cover, stirring occasionally • Halve or crush the radishes, trim and finely slice the scallions and the top leafy half of the mint, then toss it all in a bowl with the extra virgin olive oil and vinegar, and season to taste

Drain the bulgur and tip into a large serving bowl, then mash and mix in the preserved lemons and arrange the broccoli on top • Toss the sunflower seeds in the chicken pan, then slice the chicken and add to the salad, scattering over the seeds and snipping over the sprouted cress • Serve dolloped with the yogurt and drizzles of harissa, with lemon wedges on the side

SIZZLING CHICKEN FAJITAS
GRILLED PEPPERS, SALSA, RICE & BEANS

SERVES 4 | 610 CALORIES

Salsa

1 dried smoked chipotle
   or ancho chile
2 scallions
1 ripe large tomato
½ bunch of fresh cilantro
1 fresh red chile
2 limes
2 tsp balsamic vinegar
1 tbsp reduced-sodium soy sauce

Fajitas

2 mixed-color bell peppers
1 red onion
2 x 7-oz skinless boneless chicken
   breasts
1 heaping tsp sweet smoked
   paprika, plus extra to serve
olive oil

Rice & beans

1 x 14-oz can of mixed beans
½ tsp cumin seeds
1 fresh red chile
1 x 8-oz package of ready-made
   wholegrain brown rice
1 lemon

To serve

4 wholewheat flour tortillas
¼ cup fat-free plain yogurt
¾ oz feta cheese

*Ingredients out • Kettle boiled • Blender • Grill pan, high heat
• Medium frying pan, medium-high heat • Large saucepan, medium heat*

START COOKING

Tear the dried chile into the blender and just cover with boiling water to rehydrate • Trim and add the scallions with the tomato, cilantro stalks, fresh chile, juice of 1 lime, the balsamic and soy sauce, pop the lid on and leave to sit • Remove the stalks and seeds from the peppers, then tear up and place on the grill pan • Peel, quarter and add the red onion, season with salt and pepper, then let it char nicely all over

On a large sheet of parchment paper, toss the chicken with salt, pepper and the paprika • Fold over the paper, then bash and flatten the chicken to ¾-inch thick with a rolling pin • Put into the frying pan with 1 tablespoon of oil, turning after 3 or 4 minutes, until golden and cooked through • Drain and rinse the beans, then put into the large saucepan with 1 tablespoon of oil, the cumin seeds and the whole fresh chile • Toss regularly for a couple of minutes until the beans are crispy-skinned

Whiz the contents of the blender until smooth, then pour into a little serving bowl • Stir the rice and the juice of 1 lemon into the beans to warm through • Transfer the charred veg to a board, then merely warm the tortillas on the grill pan • Slice the chicken and serve with the charred veg, rice and beans, tortillas and lime wedges • Dollop yogurt over the veg, then sprinkle everything with crumbled feta and the cilantro leaves

STICKY KICKING CHICKEN
WATERMELON RADISH SALAD & CRUNCHY NOODLES

Ingredients out • Kettle boiled • Large frying pan, high heat • Medium frying pan, medium heat • Blender

Salad

7 oz thin rice noodles
Asian sesame oil
1½ lbs watermelon
2 little gem lettuces or hearts
   of romaine
1 handful of radishes
½ bunch of fresh mint
½ bunch of fresh cilantro

Chicken

8 skinless boneless chicken thighs
1 tbsp Chinese five-spice powder
olive oil
2 tbsp sweet red chili sauce
2 tbsp raw sesame seeds

Dressing

2 tbsp reduced-sodium soy sauce
1 tbsp fish sauce
½–1 fresh red chile
½ a thumb-sized piece of gingerroot
2 scallions
2 limes
1 small clove garlic

START COOKING

In a bowl, fully submerge the noodles in boiling water • On a large sheet of parchment paper, toss the chicken with salt, pepper and the five-spice • Fold over the paper, then bash and flatten the chicken to ¾-inch thick with a rolling pin • Put into the large frying pan with 1 tablespoon of olive oil, turning after 3 or 4 minutes, until nicely charred and cooked through • Drain the noodles and toss with 1 tablespoon of sesame oil on a big serving platter • Put ¼ of the noodles into the medium frying pan, tossing regularly until nice and crunchy

Remove the watermelon skin, cut the flesh into erratic chunks and add to the platter • Trim the lettuces and cut into small wedges, halve the radishes, finely slice the top leafy half of the mint and most of the top leafy half of the cilantro, and scatter over the platter • Put the cilantro stalks into the blender with the soy and fish sauces, chile, peeled ginger, trimmed scallions, a splash of water, 1 tablespoon of sesame oil and the lime juice • Squash in the unpeeled garlic through a garlic press, then whiz until smooth

Drain away any excess fat from the chicken pan, put back on the heat, drizzle with the sweet chili sauce and toss with the sesame seeds • Pour the dressing over the salad and toss gently with clean fingers until well coated, then break over the crispy noodles • Transfer the chicken to a board and serve with an extra sprinkling of cilantro leaves

MEXICAN CHICKEN
WICKED MOLE SAUCE, RICE & VEG

SERVES 4 | 625 CALORIES

Ingredients out • *Kettle boiled* • *Lidded casserole pan or Dutch oven, medium heat* • *Medium lidded saucepan, medium heat* • *Blender* • *Medium frying pan, low heat*

Chicken, rice & veg

2 carrots

2 scallions

2 chicken bouillon cubes

1 red bell pepper

2 rashers of smoked bacon

a couple of sprigs of fresh thyme

1 mug (10 oz) of 10-minute
  wholegrain brown or basmati rice

4 x 4-oz skinless boneless chicken
  breasts

6 oz okra

3 ½ oz frozen peas

Mole sauce

3 scallions

2 cloves garlic

½ fresh red chile

1 dried smoked chipotle
  or ancho chile

1 pinch of cumin seeds

1 heaping tbsp smooth peanut
  butter

1 oz dark chocolate
  (62% cocoa solids, or higher)

1 heaping tsp unsweetened cocoa
  powder

a 1-inch piece of banana

1 lemon

START COOKING

Finely slice the carrots and trimmed scallions, then put into the casserole pan with 2 cups of boiling water and crumble in the bouillon cubes • Seed the pepper, cut into 8, then add to the broth with the bacon and thyme sprigs and put the lid on • Put 1 mug of rice and 2 mugs of boiling water into the medium saucepan with a pinch of salt and cover with a lid, stirring occasionally

Trim and add the scallions, peeled garlic and chiles to the blender with the cumin seeds, peanut butter, a couple of splashes of boiling water, salt and pepper, then blitz until fine • Put into the frying pan, boil, then simmer • Add the chicken, okra and peas to the casserole pan until the chicken is cooked through, replace the lid

Scrape the mixture from the frying pan back into the blender and add the chocolate, cocoa, peeled banana and lemon juice, then whiz until silky smooth and season until it's incredible • Fluff up the rice, finely slice the chicken and serve with the mole sauce, veg and broth

GORGEOUS GREEK CHICKEN
HERBY VEGETABLE COUSCOUS & TZATZIKI

Ingredients out • Kettle boiled • Large frying pan, medium-high heat
• Food processor (metal blade)

Couscous
1 mug (10 oz) of couscous
2 mixed-color bell peppers
1 fresh red chile
4 scallions
½ bunch of fresh dill
7 oz fresh or frozen peas
1 small handful of black olives
  (with pits)
2 tbsp extra virgin olive oil
1½ oz feta cheese

Chicken
2 x 7-oz skinless boneless chicken
  breasts
1 heaping tsp dried oregano
1 tsp ground allspice
1 lemon
olive oil

Tzatziki
½ English cucumber
1 cup fat-free plain yogurt
½ lemon
½ bunch of fresh mint

START COOKING

Put 1 mug of couscous and 2 mugs of boiling water into a bowl with a pinch of salt and cover • On a large sheet of parchment paper, toss the chicken with salt, pepper, the oregano, allspice and finely grated lemon zest • Fold over the paper, then bash and flatten the chicken to ¾-inch thick with a rolling pin • Put into the frying pan with 2 tablespoons of olive oil, turning after 3 or 4 minutes, until golden and cooked through

Using a box grater, coarsely grate the cucumber • Sprinkle it with a good pinch of salt, then squeeze and scrunch with clean hands to get rid of the excess salty water • Pop in a bowl with the yogurt, juice of ½ a lemon and a pinch of pepper, finely chop and add the top leafy half of the mint, then mix together • Remove the stalk and seeds from the peppers and chile, then pulse in the processor with the trimmed scallions and the dill until finely chopped • Scatter over a large tray or platter

Add the peas to the veg (if using frozen peas, blanch them in boiling water for a couple of minutes first), pit and tear over the olives, then squeeze over the juice of the zested lemon and add the extra virgin olive oil • Fluff up and scatter over the couscous, toss well and season to taste • Move the cooked chicken to a board, slice it up, then lay it around the couscous • Crumble over the feta and serve with the tzatziki

ROSEMARY CHICKEN
GRILLED POLENTA & PORCINI TOMATO SAUCE

Ingredients out • Kettle boiled • Blender • Medium lidded saucepan, medium heat • Grill pan, high heat • Frying pan, medium heat

Sauce

1 big pinch of dried porcini
   mushrooms
14 oz ripe vine tomatoes
1 heaping tbsp tomato paste
½ fresh red chile
1 bunch of fresh basil
2 cloves garlic

Chicken & polenta

1 lb ready-made polenta
olive oil
1 bunch of asparagus (10 oz)
2 x 7-oz skinless boneless chicken
   breasts
a few sprigs of fresh rosemary
½ tbsp fennel seeds
¾ oz Parmesan cheese
4 rashers of smoked bacon
   or pancetta
6 oz oyster mushrooms
4 large handfuls of baby spinach
balsamic vinegar

START COOKING

Put the porcini in the blender with ⅔ cup of boiling water, the tomatoes, tomato paste, chile and basil, squash in the unpeeled garlic through a garlic press and blitz until smooth • Pour the tomato sauce into the medium saucepan and boil for 8 minutes, stirring occasionally • Cut the polenta into 8 slices, rub with salt, pepper and 1 teaspoon of oil and place on the grill pan, flipping over when charred and placing the trimmed asparagus on top of the polenta to steam

On a large sheet of parchment paper, toss the chicken with salt, pepper, the rosemary leaves, fennel seeds and finely grated Parmesan • Fold the paper over, then bash and flatten the chicken to ¾-inch thick with a rolling pin • Put into the frying pan with 1 tablespoon of oil, turning after 3 or 4 minutes, until golden and cooked through • Toss the bacon or pancetta and mushrooms into the pan when you turn the chicken

Season the sauce to taste, pour onto a nice serving platter and top with the polenta slices and asparagus • Transfer the chicken, bacon or pancetta and mushrooms to a board while you quickly wilt the spinach in the frying pan • Season the spinach to taste and add to the platter • Slice the chicken and arrange on top with the bacon or pancetta and mushrooms, then drizzle everything with the balsamic

WARM CHICKEN LIVER SALAD
LITTLE WELSH "RAREBITES"

SERVES 4 | 607 CALORIES

Ingredients out • Oven broiler at full whack • Food processor (fine slicer)
• Large frying pan, medium heat

"Rarebites"

1 ciabatta loaf
3 ½ oz Cheddar cheese
¼ cup fat-free plain yogurt
2 tsp grainy mustard
1 tbsp Worcestershire sauce
Tabasco

Salad

1 small red onion
½ English cucumber
1 carrot
1 lemon
2 tbsp extra virgin olive oil
½ bunch of fresh Italian parsley
7 oz mixed salad leaves
1½ oz alfalfa sprouts
balsamic vinegar
½ oz feta cheese

Livers

2 rashers of smoked bacon
olive oil
14 oz chicken livers,
   cleaned and trimmed
2 sprigs of fresh rosemary
1 tsp marmalade
½ cup Marsala
2 tbsp fat-free plain yogurt

START COOKING

Cut the ciabatta into 8 thick slices • Put them on a large baking sheet and lightly toast under the broiler on both sides • Finely grate the Cheddar into a bowl and mix with the yogurt, mustard, Worcestershire sauce and a few drips of Tabasco • Spoon over the toasts and return to the broiler on the middle shelf, removing when golden and crisp (keep an eye on them)

Peel the onion, then finely slice in the processor with the cucumber and carrot • Tip into a bowl, squeeze over the lemon juice, add the extra virgin olive oil and season with salt and pepper, then tear over the top leafy half of the parsley • Turn the heat under the frying pan up to high, then slice the bacon and put into the pan with 1 tablespoon of olive oil, the chicken livers and rosemary leaves • Toss regularly for 3 minutes, season with salt and pepper, add the marmalade and Marsala, carefully light it with a match (if you want), let the flames subside, and cook until sticky, then remove from the heat and swirl in the yogurt

Toss the salad leaves and alfalfa sprouts with the dressed sliced veg, drizzle with balsamic and spread over a large platter • Crumble over the feta and arrange the "rarebites" around the edge • Serve with the pan of chicken livers on the side

THAI CHICKEN LAKSA
MILDLY SPICED NOODLE SQUASH BROTH

Ingredients out • Kettle boiled • Grill pan, high heat
• Large lidded saucepan, high heat • Food processor (coarse grater & metal blade)

Chicken

4 skinless boneless chicken thighs
1 heaping tsp Chinese five-spice
   powder
1 tbsp honey
1 tbsp raw sesame seeds
1 fresh red chile

Laksa

1 chicken or vegetable bouillon
   cube
1 butternut squash (neck end only)
2 cloves garlic
1 thumb-sized piece of gingerroot
1 fresh red chile
1 tsp turmeric
½ bunch of scallions
1 heaping tsp smooth peanut butter
4 dried kaffir lime leaves
½ bunch of fresh cilantro
1 tbsp Asian sesame oil
1 tbsp reduced-sodium soy sauce
1 tbsp fish sauce
10 oz medium rice noodles
2 bunches of asparagus (1¼ lbs)
1 x 14-oz can of light coconut milk
3 limes

START COOKING

On a large sheet of parchment paper, toss the chicken with salt, pepper and the five-spice • Fold over the paper, then bash and flatten the chicken to ¾-inch thick with a rolling pin • Place on the hot grill pan, turning after 3 or 4 minutes, until nicely charred and cooked through • Pour about 3 ¼ cups of boiling water into the large saucepan and crumble in the bouillon cube

Trim the stalk off the squash, roughly chop the neck end (don't peel, and keep the seed end for another day), then grate and tip into the boiling broth • Swap to the metal blade in the processor and add the peeled garlic and ginger, the chile, turmeric, trimmed scallions, peanut butter, dried lime leaves, cilantro stalks (reserving the leaves), sesame oil, and soy and fish sauces • Blitz to a paste, then tip into the broth and add the noodles

Trim the asparagus and cut in half • Add to the pan, pour in the coconut milk, and as soon as it boils, taste, correct the seasoning with soy sauce and lime juice, then turn the heat off • Drizzle the honey over the charred chicken, squeeze over the juice of 1 lime, scatter with the sesame seeds and toss to coat • Serve with the laksa and lime wedges, sprinkling everything with the cilantro leaves and slices of fresh chile

BLACKENED CHICKEN
SAN FRAN QUINOA SALAD

SERVES 4 | 617 CALORIES

Ingredients out • Kettle boiled • Medium lidded saucepan, medium-high heat • Food processor (metal blade) • Large frying pan, high heat

Quinoa salad

1 mug (10 oz) of quinoa
1 fresh red or yellow chile
2 large handfuls of baby spinach
4 scallions
1 bunch of fresh cilantro
1 bunch of fresh mint
1 ripe large mango
2 limes
2 tbsp extra virgin olive oil
1 ripe avocado
1 ¾ oz feta cheese
1 cup sprouted cress

Chicken

2 x 7-oz skinless boneless chicken breasts
1 heaping tsp ground allspice
1 heaping tsp smoked paprika
olive oil
2 mixed-color bell peppers

To serve

¼ cup fat-free plain yogurt

START COOKING

Put the quinoa into the saucepan and generously cover with boiling water and the lid • Put the chile, spinach, trimmed scallions and cilantro (reserving a few leaves) into the processor, tear in the top leafy half of the mint, then blitz until finely chopped • On a large sheet of parchment paper, toss the chicken with salt, pepper, the allspice and paprika • Fold over the paper, then bash and flatten the chicken to ¾-inch thick with a rolling pin • Put into the frying pan with 1 tablespoon of olive oil, turning after 3 or 4 minutes, until blackened and cooked through

Seed the peppers, cut each one into 8 strips, and add to the frying pan, tossing regularly • Peel and cut the mango into chunks (check out: *www. jamieoliver.com/how-to* for a video of how to do this) • Drain the quinoa and rinse under the cold tap, then drain well again and tip onto a serving board or platter • Toss with the blitzed spinach mixture, squeeze over the lime juice, add the extra virgin olive oil, mix well and season to taste

Sprinkle the mango chunks and cooked peppers over the quinoa • Halve and pit the avocado, then use a teaspoon to scoop curls of it over the salad • Slice up the chicken, toss the slices in any juices and add to the salad • Crumble over the feta, scatter over the remaining cilantro leaves and snip over the cress • Serve with dollops of yogurt

GOLDEN CHICKEN
BRAISED GREENS & POTATO GRATIN

*Ingredients out • Kettle boiled • Oven broiler on high • Food processor (fine slicer)
• Medium lidded saucepan, high heat • Large high-sided roasting pan,
high heat • Large frying pan, medium-high heat*

Gratin

1½ lbs potatoes
3 onions
olive oil
1 chicken bouillon cube
½ bunch of fresh sage
⅓ cup heavy cream
1 oz Parmesan cheese

Chicken

4 x 4-oz skinless boneless chicken
   breasts
a few sprigs of fresh rosemary
2 rashers of smoked bacon

Greens

7 oz baby leeks
4 large handfuls of baby spinach
7 oz frozen peas

START COOKING

Finely slice the potatoes in the processor, then tip into the medium saucepan and cover with boiling water and the lid • Peel the onions, finely slice in the processor, then tip into the roasting pan with 2 tablespoons of oil, crumble in the bouillon cube and season with salt and pepper • Tear in the sage leaves and stir regularly, adding a splash of water if they start to catch

On a large sheet of parchment paper, toss the chicken with salt, pepper and the rosemary leaves, then fold the paper over and bash and flatten the chicken to ¾-inch thick with a rolling pin • Put into the frying pan with 1 tablespoon of oil, turning after 3 or 4 minutes, until golden and cooked through • Drain the potatoes well in a colander, then tip into the onion pan, stir together and arrange in a flat layer • Pour over the cream, then finely grate over the Parmesan and pop under the broiler on the top shelf

Halve the leeks lengthways, rinse under the tap, then finely slice • Put into the empty lidded saucepan on a high heat with 1 tablespoon of oil, stirring often • Finely slice the bacon and add to the chicken pan, tossing regularly • Stir the spinach and peas into the leeks and once the spinach has wilted and the peas are tender, pile on a board or platter with the chicken and bacon on top • Serve with the gratin

CRISPY POLENTA CHICKEN
CAESAR SALAD

Ingredients out • *Large frying pan, medium heat*
• *Grill pan, high heat* • *Blender*

Chicken

2 x 7-oz skinless boneless chicken
   breasts
½ tsp sweet smoked paprika
2 heaping tbsp fine ground
   cornmeal
olive oil

Salad

1 ciabatta loaf
1 clove garlic
2 red endives
4 slices of smoked bacon
   or pancetta
1 large head of romaine lettuce
10 ripe cherry or grape tomatoes
2 large roasted red peppers
   (from a jar)
balsamic vinegar
1 cup sprouted cress

Dressing

1 clove garlic
2 lemons
1½ oz Parmesan cheese,
   plus extra to serve
4 anchovy fillets
¼ cup fat-free plain yogurt
1 splash of Worcestershire sauce
1 tbsp red wine vinegar
1 tsp English mustard
½ bunch of fresh basil

START COOKING

On a large sheet of parchment paper, toss the chicken with salt, pepper, the paprika and cornmeal • Fold over the paper, then bash and flatten the chicken to roughly ¾-inch thick with a rolling pin • Put into the frying pan with 1 tablespoon of oil, turning after 3 or 4 minutes, until golden and cooked through • Cut 4 thick slices of ciabatta, place on the grill pan, and remove when nicely charred on both sides

Squash the unpeeled garlic through a garlic press into the blender • Squeeze in the lemon juice, crumble in the Parmesan and add the rest of the dressing ingredients • Blitz until smooth, then season to taste • Rub the toasts with a halved garlic clove and cut into thick strips • Quarter the endives and add to the grill pan with the bacon or pancetta to char for a couple of minutes

Roughly slice the lettuce and arrange over a large serving board or platter • Scatter over the ciabatta slices, halve the tomatoes and slice the peppers, then add to the board • Toss the endives in a splash of balsamic and arrange on top • Slice the chicken, lay it around the salad, drizzle with the dressing, crumble over the crispy bacon or pancetta and snip over the sprouted cress • Use a vegetable peeler to shave over a little extra Parmesan, if you like

SPICED CHICKEN
BACON, ASPARAGUS & SPINACH LENTILS

SERVES 4 | 616 CALORIES

Ingredients out • Food processor (metal blade) • Oven at 350°F • Large lidded saucepan, medium heat • Large frying pan, medium heat

Lentils
1 onion
1 carrot
2 sprigs of fresh rosemary
olive oil
2 x 19-oz cans of lentils
1 ripe tomato
4 large handfuls baby spinach
1 tsp red wine vinegar
¼ cup fat-free plain yogurt

Chicken
4 x 4-oz skinless boneless chicken
  breasts
½ tsp cayenne pepper
4 cloves garlic
1 handful of fresh thyme,
  rosemary and/or bay leaves
4 rashers of smoked bacon
  or pancetta
1 bunch of asparagus (10 oz)

To serve
crusty bread

START COOKING

Peel and halve the onion and carrot, then blitz in the processor with the rosemary leaves until fine • Put into the large saucepan with 1 tablespoon of oil, tossing regularly • On a large sheet of parchment paper, toss the chicken with salt, pepper and the cayenne, then fold the paper over and bash and flatten to ¾-inch thick with a rolling pin • Put into the frying pan with 1 tablespoon of oil, the unpeeled whole garlic cloves and a handful of fresh herbs, turning after 3 or 4 minutes, until golden and cooked through

Stir the canned lentils (and their juices) into the veg pan with the roughly chopped tomato and put the lid on • Pop the bread into the oven to warm through • Roughly chop the spinach in the processor and add to the lentils with the red wine vinegar • When the lentils are boiling and the spinach wilted, season to taste • Add the bacon or pancetta and trimmed asparagus to the chicken pan and fry until golden and crispy

Tip the lentils onto a platter, then swirl through most of the yogurt • Remove the chicken to a board, cut in half at an angle, and serve on top of the lentils with the crispy bacon or pancetta, asparagus and garlic • Dollop over the remaining yogurt, then serve with the crusty bread to mop up the juices

CRISPY DUCK
HOISIN LETTUCE PARCELS

SERVES 4 | 738 CALORIES

Ingredients out • Kettle boiled • Small lidded saucepan, medium heat
• Large frying pan, medium heat

Parcels

4 nests of fine egg noodles
1 large head of iceberg lettuce
1 tbsp Asian sesame oil
¼ cup hoisin sauce
4 limes
1 clove garlic
1 package (11 oz) of silken tofu
1 bunch of baby radishes
5 sprigs of fresh cilantro
1 cup sprouted cress
sweet red chili sauce

Duck

2 x 7-oz duck breasts, skin on
1 heaping tsp Chinese five-spice
  powder
olive oil
1 fresh red chile
2 scallions
1 handful of unsalted raw
  cashew nuts
2 tbsp raw sesame seeds
1 tsp honey

START COOKING

Put the noodles into the small saucepan and cover with boiling water and the lid • Cut the duck into ½-inch dice, toss with salt, pepper and the five-spice, then put into the frying pan with 1 tablespoon of olive oil and toss regularly • Cut the lettuce in half through the stalk, remove the stalk, then separate the leaves into cups and arrange on a large clean tray or platter

Drain the noodles and toss with the sesame oil, then divide them between the lettuce cups • Finely slice the chile and trimmed scallions • When the duck is nice and golden, pour away any excess fat, then stir in the chile, scallions, cashews and sesame seeds, and toss regularly

Put the hoisin sauce into a bowl, squeeze in the juice from 3 limes, squash in the unpeeled garlic through a garlic press and mix together • Drizzle the duck with the honey, shake the pan to coat, then tip it evenly over the lettuce cups • Cut the tofu into rough 1-inch chunks and sprinkle it in and around the lettuce cups • Scatter over the baby radishes and cilantro leaves, then snip over the sprouted cress • Drizzle the hoisin dressing over everything from a height and drizzle each piece of tofu with a little sweet chili sauce • Serve with lime wedges

CHILI CON CARNE
MEATBALLS

SERVES 4 | 437 CALORIES

Bulgur
1 mug (10 oz) of bulgur
1 preserved lemon
1 cinnamon stick

Meatballs
14 oz lean ground beef
1 heaping tsp garam masala
olive oil
3 roasted red peppers (from a jar)
4 scallions
1 tsp smoked paprika
3 ¼ cups passata
1 bunch of fresh cilantro
1 x 14-oz can of red kidney beans
1 pinch of cumin seeds
¼ cup fat-free plain yogurt
1 lime

Grilled chiles
4 fresh chiles

Ingredients out • Kettle boiled • Oven broiler on high • Medium lidded saucepan, high heat • Large frying pan, high heat • Blender • Medium frying pan, medium heat

START COOKING

Put 1 mug of bulgur, 2 mugs of boiling water, the preserved lemon and the cinnamon stick into the medium saucepan and cover, stirring occasionally • With clean hands, scrunch the ground beef with salt, pepper and the garam masala • Divide the mixture into 4, then with wet hands quickly shape each piece into 4 balls, placing them into the frying pan as you roll them and adding 1 tablespoon of oil, toss regularly

Blitz the peppers, half the trimmed scallions, the paprika, passata, half the cilantro and a pinch of salt and pepper in the blender until smooth, then pour into the medium frying pan (swirl a good splash of water around the blender and pour into the pan) and turn the heat up to high • Prick the chiles and put under the broiler to blacken all over, then remove

Rinse and drain the beans, then add to the meatballs with the cumin seeds • Use tongs to transfer the meatballs straight into the pan of sauce, leaving the beans behind • Finely slice the remaining trimmed scallions • Stir the beans into the sauce • Remove the cinnamon stick, then mash the lemon into the bulgur and serve with the meatball sauce, dollops of yogurt, the charred chiles and wedges of lime, scattered with the remaining scallions and cilantro leaves

BRITISH BURGERS
SHRED SALAD, PICKLES & THINGS

SERVES 4 | 532 CALORIES

Ingredients out • Oven at 250°F • Large frying pan, medium heat • Food processor (coarse grater)

Burgers

1 lb lean ground beef
1 heaping tsp grainy mustard
1 swig of quality beer or ale
olive oil
4 wholewheat buns
2 tbsp fat-free plain yogurt
Worcestershire sauce
1 ripe beefsteak tomato
2–4 gherkins
tomato ketchup, to serve

Salad

2 carrots
¼ head of white cabbage
   (roughly 8 oz)
1 pear
1 small red onion
2 tbsp extra virgin olive oil
1 tbsp red wine vinegar
2 oz arugula

START COOKING

Put the ground beef into a bowl with salt, pepper, the mustard and the beer or ale, then with clean hands scrunch and mix together • Divide the mixture into 4 and with wet hands shape into patties about 1-inch thick, then put into the pan with 1 tablespoon of olive oil, turning when crispy and golden, and pushing down on them with a slotted spatula so they're in good contact with the pan

Place the buns into the oven • Put the yogurt into a small bowl, add a good splash of Worcestershire sauce, then stir and ripple it together • Slice the tomato and gherkins on a nice serving board

In the processor, grate the trimmed carrots, cabbage, pear (stalk removed) and peeled red onion • Put the extra virgin olive oil and vinegar into a serving bowl, tip in the grated veg, toss together and season to taste, then mix in the arugula • Get the buns out of the oven, cut them in half and dollop with ketchup • Top with a slice of tomato and the burgers, then let everyone build their own at the table

BEEF STROGANOFF
FLUFFY RICE, RED ONION & PARSLEY PICKLE

SERVES 4 | 625 CALORIES

Ingredients out • *Kettle boiled* • *Medium lidded saucepan, medium heat*
• *Food processor (fine slicer)* • *Large frying pan, high heat*

Rice

1 mug (10 oz) of 10-minute
  wholegrain brown or basmati rice
½ bunch of fresh thyme
4 large handfuls of baby spinach

Pickle

2 small red onions
1 handful of gherkins and juice
1 bunch of fresh Italian parsley

Stroganoff

10 oz mixed mushrooms
olive oil
3 cloves garlic
2 x 7-oz sirloin steaks,
  fat removed
1 heaping tsp sweet paprika
1 lemon
1 swig of brandy
¼ cup fat-free plain yogurt
1 swig of reduced-fat (2%) milk

START COOKING

Put 1 mug of rice, 2 mugs of boiling water, the thyme leaves and a pinch of salt and pepper into the medium saucepan and put the lid on, stirring occasionally • Peel the onions, then finely slice them with the gherkins in the processor and tip into a bowl • Finely slice the parsley stalks and roughly chop the leaves, then toss into the bowl with a swig of gherkin vinegar and a pinch of salt, scrunching together well

Tear or slice the mushrooms into the frying pan with 2 tablespoons of oil, then squash in the unpeeled garlic through a garlic press and add two-thirds of the parsley pickle, stirring regularly • Slice the steaks about ½-inch thick and toss with salt, pepper, the paprika and the finely grated lemon zest • Tip the mushrooms onto a plate, then add 2 tablespoons of oil and the steak to the pan in one layer, turning when golden

Add the spinach to the rice pan and replace the lid • Add the brandy to the steak, carefully light it with a match (if you want), let the flames subside, then return the mushrooms to the pan with the yogurt and milk and bring to a boil • Transfer the wilted spinach to a nice serving platter, then fluff up and scatter the rice over the top • Spoon over the stroganoff, squeeze and drain the remaining pickle, then scatter over from a height

SIZZLING BEEF STEAK
HOISIN SHRIMP & NOODLE BOWLS

SERVES 4 | 653 CALORIES

Ingredients out • *Kettle boiled* • *Wok, high heat* • *Large frying pan, high heat* • *Food processor (metal blade)* • *Medium lidded saucepan, high heat*

Bowls

2 tbsp unsalted blanched peanuts
2 tbsp raw sesame seeds
½–1 fresh red chile
1 thumb-sized piece of gingerroot
2 scallions
1 bunch of fresh cilantro
4 nests of egg noodles
2 cloves garlic
3 ½ oz raw peeled tiger shrimp
2 ½ oz beansprouts
¼ cup hoisin sauce
2 tbsp reduced-sodium soy sauce
2 limes
1 head of romaine lettuce
4 radishes
1 cup sprouted cress

Beef

2 x 7-oz sirloin steaks,
  fat removed
1 tbsp Chinese five-spice powder
2 tbsp Asian sesame oil
8 oz oyster mushrooms

START COOKING

Toast the peanuts and sesame seeds in the dry wok, tossing often until golden, then tip into a small bowl and put aside, leaving the wok on the heat • Rub the steaks all over with salt, pepper and the five-spice, then put into the frying pan with half the sesame oil • Turn the steaks every minute until cooked to your liking, adding the mushrooms after a couple of minutes and removing the steaks to a board when done • Finely chop the chile, peeled ginger, trimmed scallions and half the cilantro in the processor

Half-fill the saucepan with boiling salted water and add the noodles, then put the lid on • Put the remaining sesame oil into the wok, add the chopped veg and squash in the unpeeled garlic through a garlic press • Toss for a minute, add the shrimp and beansprouts, toss for another minute, then add the hoisin and soy sauces, the juice of 1 lime and the rest of the cilantro leaves

Use tongs to drain and transfer the noodles straight into the wok and toss in, loosening with a splash of cooking water if needed • Season to taste and divide between 4 bowls • Trim the lettuce, break the leaves apart and poke a couple of leaves into each bowl with a halved radish • Snip over the sprouted cress and sprinkle with the toasted nuts and seeds • Cut the steaks into ½-inch slices and serve with the crispy mushrooms and lime wedges

BEEF KOFTA CURRY
FLUFFY RICE, BEANS & PEAS

Ingredients out • Kettle boiled • Large frying pan, high heat • Medium lidded casserole pan or Dutch oven, high heat • Blender

Curry

½ x 19-oz can of lentils
  (drained and rinsed)
1 heaping tsp garam masala
14 oz lean ground beef
olive oil
3 ripe tomatoes
1 thumb-sized piece of gingerroot
2 scallions
1 fresh red chile
1 bunch of fresh cilantro
1 tsp turmeric
1 tsp honey
2 heaping tsp Patak's rogan josh
  (medium) curry paste
½ x 14-oz can of light coconut milk
¼ cup fat-free plain yogurt,
  to serve
1 lemon

Rice

1 mug (10 oz) of 10-minute
  wholegrain brown or basmati rice
5 cardamom pods
7 oz green or yellow beans
7 oz frozen peas
2 uncooked pappadams

START COOKING

Put the lentils into a bowl with salt, pepper, the garam masala and ground beef, then mix and scrunch together with clean hands • Divide the mixture in half, then with wet hands quickly squeeze and mold each half into 6 fat fingers • Put them into the frying pan with 1 tablespoon of oil, turning when golden

Put 1 mug of rice, 2 mugs of boiling water and the cardamom pods into the casserole pan, then halve and add the beans and put the lid on • Squash the tomatoes into the blender, add the peeled ginger, trimmed scallions, half the chile, the cilantro stalks, turmeric, honey, curry paste and coconut milk, then blitz until combined • Pour into the kofta pan, bring to a boil, then simmer and season to taste

Take the lid off the rice, add the peas, mix it all up and give it just a few more minutes • Crack up the uncooked pappadams and pop them in the microwave (on high) for a minute or two to puff up • Finely slice the remaining chile and the cilantro leaves and scatter them over the curry, dollop with yogurt, then serve with lemon wedges, pappadams and the rice, beans and peas

SEARED ASIAN BEEF
BEST NOODLE SALAD & GINGER DRESSING

SERVES 4 | 585 CALORIES

Ingredients out • Kettle boiled • Large frying pan, high heat

Salad

2 oz unsalted raw cashew nuts

1 tbsp unsalted raw sunflower
  seeds

2 tbsp raw sesame seeds

7 oz fine rice noodles

1 head of romaine lettuce

1 large carrot

1 bunch of radishes

½ English cucumber

1 big bunch of fresh cilantro

3 scallions

1 cup sprouted cress

1 large handful of alfalfa sprouts

Steak

1 x 1-lb sirloin steak (cut ½-inch
  thick)

2 tsp Chinese five-spice powder

olive oil

Dressing

3 tbsp pickled ginger

2 limes

1 tbsp fish sauce

1 tbsp reduced-sodium soy sauce

1 tbsp Asian sesame oil

½ fresh red chile

START COOKING

Toast the cashews, sunflower and sesame seeds in the frying pan, tossing regularly until golden, then tip into a bowl and return the pan to high heat • Put the noodles into another bowl with a pinch of salt and cover with boiling water • Rub the steak with salt, pepper and the five-spice, and put into the frying pan with 1 tablespoon of olive oil, turning every minute until cooked to your liking

In another bowl, mix together the pickled ginger and its juice, the juice of 1 to 2 limes, the fish and soy sauces and sesame oil, then finely slice and add the chile • Trim the lettuce and break the leaves apart, shredding any larger ones, then scatter over a large board • Coarsely grate over the trimmed carrot, using a box grater • Halve the radishes, roughly chop the cucumber and the top leafy half of the cilantro and trim and finely slice the scallions

Pile all the veg on the board, snip over the sprouted cress and scatter over the alfalfa sprouts • Drain the noodles, rinse and drain again, then add them to the board • When the steak is done, move it to a board to rest, then slice and place on top of the salad, pouring over any resting juices • Scatter over the nuts and serve the dressing on the side, with any remaining lime wedges

GRILLED STEAK
RATATOUILLE & SAFFRON RICE

SERVES 4 | 593 CALORIES

Ingredients out • Kettle boiled • Grill pan, high heat • Small lidded saucepan, medium heat • Shallow lidded casserole pan or Dutch oven, medium heat

Ratatouille
1 zucchini
1 small eggplant
2 mixed-color bell peppers
1 red onion
1 heaping tsp harissa
2 anchovy fillets
2–4 cloves garlic
3 ¼ cups passata
1 tbsp balsamic vinegar
½ bunch of fresh basil
2 tbsp fat-free plain yogurt

Rice
1 mug (10 oz) of 10-minute
  wholegrain brown or basmati rice
1 good pinch of saffron
½ lemon

Steaks
2 x 8-oz sirloin steaks,
  fat removed
1 tsp sweet paprika
olive oil
½ bunch of fresh Italian parsley
1 heaping tsp Dijon mustard
1 tbsp extra virgin olive oil
½ lemon

START COOKING

Halve the zucchini lengthways, slice the eggplant ½-inch thick and place both on the grill pan, turning when charred • Put 1 mug of rice, 2 mugs of boiling water, the saffron, lemon half and a pinch of salt into the small saucepan, cover and cook until fluffy, stirring occasionally • Tear the seeds and stalks out of the peppers, then roughly chop with the peeled red onion and put into the casserole pan with the harissa, anchovies and 1 teaspoon of their oil • Squash in the unpeeled garlic through a garlic press and stir regularly

Remove the charred zucchini and eggplant from the grill pan, leaving it on the heat, and roughly chop them on a board • Add them to the casserole pan along with the passata and balsamic, and boil with the lid on • Rub the steaks with salt, the paprika and 1 teaspoon of olive oil and place on the hot grill pan, turning every minute until cooked to your liking

On a board, finely slice the parsley stalks and roughly chop the leaves • Add the mustard and extra virgin olive oil, season with salt and pepper and squeeze over the lemon juice, then mix together and spread over the board • When the steaks are done, transfer them to the board, turn them in the dressing, then slice • Tear the top leafy half of the basil into the ratatouille, season to taste, and serve with yogurt and saffron rice

BEEF CHIMICHURRI
BABY POTATOES & CRUNCH SALAD

SERVES 4 | 613 CALORIES

Ingredients out • Kettle boiled • Medium lidded saucepan, high heat • Blender • Large frying pan, high heat

Potatoes

1½ lbs baby white potatoes
1 lemon
1 tsp dried dill

Beef

4 cloves garlic
6 scallions
2 heaping tsp dried oregano
½ fresh red chile
1 fresh bay leaf
1 bunch of fresh cilantro
2–3 tbsp red wine vinegar
2 x 8-oz sirloin steaks,
    fat removed
olive oil

Salad

2 little gem lettuces or hearts
    of romaine
1 handful of ripe heirloom mixed
    tomatoes
½ bunch of fresh mint
1 cup sprouted cress
5 oz podded fresh peas
extra virgin olive oil
1 tbsp balsamic vinegar
Parmesan cheese, to serve

START COOKING

Put the baby potatoes and whole lemon into the medium saucepan, then cover with boiling salted water and the lid • Peel the garlic and put into the blender with the trimmed and halved scallions, the oregano, chile, bay leaf and cilantro (reserving a few leaves) • Add the vinegar and a splash of boiling water, whiz until smooth, season to taste and pour into a bowl

Rub the steaks with salt and pepper, then put into the hot frying pan with 1 tablespoon of olive oil, turning every minute until cooked to your liking • Roughly chop the lettuces, tomatoes and the top leafy half of the mint and place on a platter, then snip over the cress and sprinkle over the raw peas • Dress with 1 tablespoon of extra virgin olive oil and the balsamic, and finish with a grating of Parmesan

Drain the potatoes and lemon, tip into a bowl and use tongs to squash the lemon juice over the potatoes, then discard • Toss with 1 tablespoon of extra virgin olive oil, salt, pepper and the dill, then transfer to the platter • Add the steaks and chimichurri sauce to the platter, sprinkle with the reserved cilantro leaves and slice at the table

STEAK, LIVER & BACON
BUBBLE & SQUEAK MASH, RED ONION GRAVY

SERVES 4 | 556 CALORIES

Mash
1½ lbs potatoes
1 lb Brussels sprouts
1 splash of reduced-fat (2%) milk

Steak
1 x 9-oz beef tenderloin steak
7 oz calves' liver slices
1 tbsp dry mustard powder
olive oil
4 rashers of smoked bacon
a few sprigs of fresh lemon thyme

Gravy
2 red onions
2 sprigs of fresh rosemary
1 heaping tsp all-purpose flour
1 tbsp blackberry jam
1 tbsp Worcestershire sauce
1 swig of smooth beer or ale
1 chicken bouillon cube

Ingredients out • Kettle boiled • Food processor (thick slicer)
• Large lidded saucepan, medium heat • Medium frying pan, high heat
• Small casserole pan or Dutch oven, high heat

START COOKING

Thickly slice the potatoes and Brussels sprouts in the processor, then tip into the large saucepan and cover with boiling salted water and the lid • Rub the steak and liver slices with salt and the mustard powder • Press and whack the steak out so it's 1¼-inch thick, then add only the steak to the frying pan with 1 tablespoon of oil, turning every minute until cooked to your liking

Peel and halve the onions, then slice them in the processor and tip into the casserole pan with 1 tablespoon of oil and the rosemary leaves, stirring regularly • Drain the veg, return them to the pan, mash with the milk, and season to taste • Stir the flour into the onions, followed by the jam, Worcestershire sauce and beer or ale, crumble in the bouillon cube and add 1¼ cups of boiling water, then season with salt and pepper and simmer

Remove the steak to a plate to rest, then add the bacon to the pan • When you flip it, add the liver slices and thyme sprigs, turning after a minute or so • Serve the mash on a nice board or platter with the liver, bacon and crispy thyme on top, slice up and add the steak and any resting juices, and serve the gravy in a pitcher on the side

KOREAN FRIED RICE
STEAK, MUSHROOMS & PICKLES

SERVES 4 | 545 CALORIES

Ingredients out • Large frying pan, medium heat
• Grill pan, high heat • Food processor (fine slicer)

Rice
2 x 8-oz packages of ready-made
    wholegrain brown rice
1 lemon

Steak & mushrooms
4 oz oyster mushrooms
Asian sesame oil
reduced-sodium soy sauce
sherry vinegar
1 clove garlic
2 x 8-oz sirloin steaks,
    fat removed

Pickle
1 English cucumber
2 scallions
superfine sugar

Garnishes
1 little gem lettuce or heart of
    romaine
1 tbsp harissa, plus extra to serve
2 large handfuls of baby spinach
2 large eggs
2 tbsp raw sesame seeds

START COOKING

Tip the cooked rice into the frying pan, squeeze over the lemon juice and stir regularly • Place the mushrooms on the grill pan, turning when charred • Put 1 tablespoon of oil, 2 tablespoons of soy sauce and 1 tablespoon of sherry vinegar in a medium bowl, squash in the unpeeled garlic through a garlic press, then mix well to create a marinade • Slice the steaks ½-inch thick

Tip the mushrooms into the bowl of marinade, then lay the steak over the grill in one layer, cook until nicely charred on one side only, then toss with the mushrooms and marinade • Finely slice the cucumber and trimmed scallions in the processor, then tip into a bowl • Add a pinch of salt and sugar, and a drizzle of soy sauce and sherry vinegar, then with clean hands scrunch everything together

Shred the lettuce and put in a little bowl, then put the harissa and spinach in similar bowls • Tip the rice into a large bowl • Add 1 teaspoon of oil to the frying pan, crack in the eggs, sprinkle over the sesame seeds, then cook for 1½ minutes on each side so that the yolks are still soft, and place on top of the rice • To serve, mix everything together like a giant salad and adjust the spice to your liking with a little extra harissa

SWEDISH MEATBALLS
CELERY ROOT & SPINACH RICE

SERVES 4 | 576 CALORIES

Ingredients out • Kettle boiled • Lidded casserole pan or Dutch oven, medium heat • Small lidded saucepan, medium heat • Medium frying pan, medium heat

Rice

1 celery root
olive oil
a few sprigs of fresh lemon thyme
1 mug (10 oz) of 10-minute
    wholegrain brown or basmati rice
4 large handfuls of baby spinach

Meatballs

7 oz lean ground beef
7 oz lean ground pork
½ bunch of fresh dill
2 tsp caraway seeds
1 swig of vodka
4 tsp cranberry jam
¼ cup heavy cream
¼ cup fat-free plain yogurt,
    to serve

START COOKING

Carefully trim the knobbly end off the celery root, remove the skin, then dice it into ½-inch pieces • Put into the casserole pan with 1 tablespoon of oil, a pinch of salt and pepper, the thyme leaves and a splash of boiling water • Put the lid on, turn the heat to high and cook, stirring regularly • Put 1 mug of rice, 2 mugs of boiling water and a pinch of salt into the small saucepan and put the lid on

Put all the ground beef and pork into a bowl with a pinch of salt and pepper, finely chop and add most of the dill, then mix and scrunch together with clean hands • Divide the mixture into 4, then pinch and quickly roll out 5 balls from each piece with wet hands • Pour 1 tablespoon of oil into the hot frying pan, add the meatballs and caraway seeds, turn the heat up to high and toss regularly until the meatballs are golden

Stir the spinach into the casserole pan, followed by the cooked rice, then season to taste • Add a good swig of vodka to the meatballs, carefully light it with a match (if you want), let the flames subside, then add the jam, cream and a few good splashes of water, and simmer • Season and serve with the rice, scattered with the remaining dill leaves and yogurt

BLACK BEAN BEEF BURGERS NOODLES & PICKLE SALAD

SERVES 4 | 558 CALORIES

Ingredients out • Kettle boiled • Medium frying pan, medium-high heat • Wok, high heat • Food processor (fine slicer)

Burgers
14 oz lean ground beef
6 tbsp black bean sauce
olive oil
1 tbsp honey
2 tbsp raw sesame seeds
1 lime

Noodles
1 chicken bouillon cube
1 thumb-sized piece of gingerroot
4 nests of egg noodles
2 mixed-color bell peppers
7 oz sugar snap peas
2 baby bok choy
5 oz mixed mushrooms
1 lime

Salad
1 x 7-oz can of water chestnuts
3 scallions
½ fresh red chile
1 lime
½ bunch of fresh cilantro
reduced-sodium soy sauce

START COOKING

Put the ground beef, half the black bean sauce and a pinch of salt and pepper into a bowl and scrunch together with your hands • Divide the mixture into 4 pieces and shape each one into a patty about 1-inch thick with wet hands • Put into the frying pan with 1 tablespoon of oil, turning when golden • Pour 2 ⅓ cups of boiling water into the wok, crumble in the bouillon cube, then peel, slice and add the ginger

Drain the water chestnuts and slice in the processor with the trimmed scallions and chile, then tip into a bowl • Add the juice of 1 lime and a pinch of salt, then scrunch and toss together • Rip off and add the top leafy half of the cilantro (reserving the stalks) and drizzle with a little soy, then put aside • Put the noodles into the wok to boil for 2 minutes, breaking them apart, then add the rest of the black bean sauce and the juice from 1 lime

Rip the seeds and stalks out of the peppers, then slice in the processor with the sugar snaps, bok choy and cilantro stalks • Tip the sliced veg into the wok, tear in the mushrooms and cook for 1 minute, then serve in a nice bowl • Sprinkle the burgers with the honey and sesame seeds and toss to coat, then transfer them to a serving board with lime wedges and the pickle salad, tossing the pickle at the last minute

STEAK MEDALLIONS
MUSHROOM SAUCE & SPRING GREENS

SERVES 4 | 663 CALORIES

Ingredients out • Kettle boiled • Casserole pan or Dutch oven, high heat • Medium frying pan, medium heat • Grill pan, high heat • Immersion blender

Mushroom sauce
1 oz dried porcini mushrooms
olive oil
8 oz mixed mushrooms
2 cloves garlic
1 good splash of brandy
¼ cup heavy cream
1 tsp truffle oil

Greens
1½ lbs baby white potatoes
½ head of Savoy cabbage
   (roughly 14 oz)
1 bunch of broccolini (7 oz)
8 oz frozen peas
1 tbsp extra virgin olive oil
½ lemon

Steak
4 x 4-oz beef tenderloin medallions
5 oz oyster mushrooms

START COOKING

Put the porcini into a small bowl and cover with boiling water • Halving any larger ones, put the baby potatoes into the casserole pan and cover with boiling salted water and the lid • Slice the cabbage 1-inch thick, add it to the pan and replace the lid • Put 1 tablespoon of olive oil into the frying pan and tear in the mixed mushrooms • Squash the unpeeled garlic through a garlic press over the top, add the porcini (reserving the liquid) and a pinch of salt and pepper, and toss regularly

Rub the steaks with salt, pepper and 1 tablespoon of olive oil, then place on the grill pan with the oyster mushrooms, turning the steaks every minute until cooked to your liking • Trim the ends off the broccolini, then add it to the casserole pan with the peas to cook for 2 minutes • Drain, toss in the extra virgin olive oil and the juice of ½ a lemon, and season to taste

Add the brandy to the mixed mushrooms, carefully light it with a match (if you want), let the flames subside, then add the cream and truffle oil and bring to a boil • Adjust the consistency with the reserved porcini liquid (discarding any gritty bits), then blend the sauce to the consistency of your liking and season to taste • Serve with the steaks, oyster mushrooms, spuds and greens

CAJUN STEAK
SMOKY BAKED BEANS & COLLARD GREENS

Greens
2 rashers of smoked bacon or
pancetta
olive oil
1 big bunch of mixed fresh herbs,
    such as thyme, rosemary and bay
    leaves
1 carrot
4 scallions
½ bunch of radishes
7 oz curly kale or collards
1 chicken bouillon cube

Beans
2 x 14-oz cans of mixed beans
1½ cups passata
1 tsp Worcestershire sauce
1 tsp Tabasco
2 tbsp tomato ketchup
2 tbsp HP sauce
1 tsp honey
1 heaping tsp English mustard,
    plus extra to serve
1½ oz Cheddar cheese

Steak
2 x 8-oz sirloin steaks, fat removed
1 tsp sweet paprika
1 tsp dried thyme

Chile vinegar
1 fresh red chile
1 bottle of white wine vinegar

Ingredients out • Kettle boiled • Oven at full whack (475°F)
• Large lidded saucepan, medium-high heat • Medium ovenproof frying pan,
medium heat • Large frying pan, high heat

START COOKING

Slice the bacon or pancetta, put it into the lidded saucepan with 1 tablespoon of oil, then pick in the herb leaves • Trim, finely slice and add the carrot, scallions and radishes, stirring regularly • Drain and rinse the beans and put into the medium frying pan with 2 tablespoons of oil to fry and crisp up

Slice the kale (if needed) and add to the saucepan, crumble in the bouillon cube and pour over 1¼ cups of boiling water, then put the lid on • Stir the remaining beans ingredients (except the cheese) into the beans pan and bring to a boil • Grate over the Cheddar, then place in the oven until golden and sizzling

Rub the steaks with salt, pepper, the paprika and thyme • Put them into the really hot large frying pan with 1 tablespoon of oil, turning every minute until cooked to your liking • Slice the chile and add to the bottle of vinegar with a couple of bay leaves, if you have them (it will keep for months), then add a drizzle to the greens before serving • Carve the steaks on a board at the table and serve with the beans, greens and a splodge of mustard

PORK

CRISPY PARMA PORK
MINTED ZUCCHINI & BROWN RICE

SERVES 4 | 582 CALORIES

Ingredients out • Large frying pan, medium heat
• Food processor (fine slicer) • Large casserole pan or Dutch oven, medium heat

Pork

14 oz pork tenderloin
1½ oz feta cheese
4 slices of Parma ham or prosciutto
olive oil
8 fresh sage leaves
balsamic vinegar

Zucchini

6 medium green and yellow zucchini
5 cloves garlic
1 fresh red chile
½ bunch of fresh mint

To serve

2 tsp sun-dried tomato paste
1 lemon
2 x 8-oz packages of ready-made
   wholegrain brown rice
¼ cup fat-free plain yogurt

START COOKING

Cut the pork into 8 even-sized medallions and make a slit in the center of each one • Cut the feta into 8 pieces and poke these into the slits in the pork, then sprinkle with a little black pepper and wrap each piece with ½ a slice of Parma ham • Flatten with your fist and put into the frying pan, ham-side down, with 1 tablespoon of oil, turning regularly until golden and cooked through

Finely slice the zucchini in the processor and add to the casserole pan with 2 tablespoons of oil • Squash in the unpeeled garlic through a garlic press and turn the heat up to high • Finely chop the chile and most of the top leafy half of the mint and add to the pan, season to taste with salt and pepper, then stir regularly until softened and delicious

Add the sage leaves to the pork pan for 30 seconds until crispy • Tip the zucchini onto a serving platter and arrange the pork and sage on top • Return the frying pan to a high heat, add a splash of water, the sun-dried tomato paste and lemon juice, then tip in the rice and warm through for 1 minute • Serve the rice drizzled with yogurt, drizzle a little balsamic over the pork, then scatter everything with the remaining mint leaves

GLAZED PORK TENDERLOIN
CAJUN-STYLE PEPPER RICE & BBQ SAUCE

SERVES 4 | 611 CALORIES

Pork
1¼ lbs pork tenderloin
1 heaping tsp ground allspice
olive oil

Rice
1 red onion
1 celery stalk
6 oz okra
2 mixed-color bell peppers
1 tsp sweet smoked paprika
1 pinch of cumin seeds
1 tsp fennel seeds
2 x 8-oz packages of ready-made
   wholegrain brown rice
1 lemon
½ bunch of fresh basil

BBQ sauce
2 cloves garlic
2 tbsp Worcestershire sauce
⅓ cup tomato ketchup
2 tbsp HP sauce
1 heaping tbsp honey
1 tbsp reduced-sodium soy sauce
1 tsp Tabasco
3 tbsp fresh apple juice

To serve
pickled veg
¼ cup fat-free plain yogurt

Ingredients out • Oven broiler on medium-high • Large frying pan, medium heat • Large casserole pan or Dutch oven, high heat

START COOKING

Score lengthways halfway through the center of the pork, open it out like a book, then flatten it slightly with your fist • Rub with salt, pepper and the allspice, then put it into the frying pan with 1 tablespoon of oil, turning when it has a dark golden crust (roughly 4 minutes) • Roughly chop the peeled onion, trimmed celery, okra and seeded peppers, putting them into the casserole pan as you go with 1 tablespoon of oil, then add the paprika, cumin and fennel seeds and 1 cup of water, stirring regularly

Squash the unpeeled garlic through a garlic press into a bowl, add all the remaining sauce ingredients and a pinch of salt, then mix well • When the pork has a good crust on both sides, transfer to a baking dish • Pour over most of the sauce and place under the broiler until the pork is cooked through • Pour the rest of the sauce into a small bowl to serve on the side

Stir the rice into the veg pan, squeeze in the lemon juice, then roughly chop and add the top leafy half of the basil and season to taste • Slice up the glazed pork at the table and serve with the extra sauce and bowls of pickled veg, such as gherkins, cauliflower, red cabbage and anything else crunchy and delicious • Dollop yogurt over the rice before serving

ULTIMATE PORK TACOS
SPICY BLACK BEANS & AVOCADO GARDEN SALAD

SERVES 4 | 582 CALORIES

Ingredients out • Large frying pan, medium-high heat • Medium frying pan, medium heat

Pork
12 oz skinless pork belly
1 heaping tsp fennel seeds
1 heaping tsp sweet smoked
  paprika

Beans
olive oil
1 good pinch of cumin seeds
3 scallions
2 cloves garlic
1 x 14-oz can of black beans

Salad
1 fresh red or green chile
2 little gem lettuces or hearts of
  romaine
½ bunch of fresh cilantro
1 ripe avocado
1 large ripe tomato
1 eating apple
reduced-sodium soy sauce
1 tbsp extra virgin olive oil
1 lime

To serve
hot chili sauce
¼ cup fat-free plain yogurt
8 corn taco shells

START COOKING

Cut the pork into ½-inch dice and tip into the large frying pan with the fennel seeds, paprika, salt and pepper, and stir regularly • Put 1 tablespoon of olive oil and the cumin seeds into the medium frying pan • Trim, slice and add the scallions, squash in the unpeeled garlic through a garlic press, then stir in the beans and their juices, and simmer

Finely slice the chile, lettuce and most of the top leafy half of the cilantro, then halve, pit, peel and chop the avocado, along with the tomato • Toss and pile all this on a platter, coarsely grating or matchsticking the apple on top • Ripple a little chili sauce through the yogurt in a small bowl

Stir, mush and season the beans to taste • Drizzle the salad with a little soy sauce, the extra virgin olive oil and lime juice, then toss together • Drain the fat from the pork pan, then serve everything straight away, with a pile of taco shells and all the other elements, sprinkled with the remaining cilantro leaves

PORK STEAKS
HUNGARIAN PEPPER SAUCE & RICE

Sauce
2 mixed-color bell peppers
1 red onion
1 carrot
1 bulb fennel
1 eating apple
olive oil
2 tsp sweet smoked paprika,
    plus extra to serve
4–5 fresh bay leaves
4 cloves garlic
2 tbsp balsamic vinegar
3 ¼ cups passata

Rice & pork
1 mug (10 oz) of 10-minute
    wholegrain brown or basmati rice
1 lb pork tenderloin
1 tsp ground coriander

To serve
2 ½ oz arugula
1 lemon
¼ cup fat-free plain yogurt

Ingredients out • *Kettle boiled* • *Food processor (thick slicer)* • *Large casserole pan or Dutch oven, medium heat* • *Medium lidded saucepan, medium heat* • *Grill pan, high heat*

START COOKING

Seed the peppers, peel and halve the onion, trim the carrot, trim and quarter the fennel (reserving any leafy tops), then slice them all in the processor with the apple • Put 2 tablespoons of oil into the casserole pan, tip in the sliced veg, add the paprika and bay leaves, squash in the unpeeled garlic through a garlic press, season with salt and pepper, and fry, stirring regularly

Put 1 mug of rice and 2 mugs of boiling water into the medium saucepan with a good pinch of salt, cover and stir occasionally • Slice the pork into 8 medallions, flatten them slightly with your fist, then rub with salt, pepper, the ground coriander and 1 teaspoon of oil, then put on the grill pan until cooked through, turning when nicely charred

Add the balsamic and passata to the peppers, season to taste and bring to a boil • Sprinkle the rice with an extra dusting of paprika • Dress the arugula with the lemon juice and a small pinch of salt, then fold most of it through the sauce • Tip the sauce onto a platter, place the charred pork on top and scatter with the remaining arugula • Drizzle with the yogurt, scatter over any reserved fennel tops and serve with the fluffy rice

JERK PORK

GRILLED CORN & CRUNCHY TORTILLA SALAD

SERVES 4 | 641 CALORIES

Ingredients out • Oven at 350°F • Grill pan, high heat • Large frying pan, high heat • Blender

Salad

4 corn cobs (husks removed)

8 small corn tortillas

1 head of romaine lettuce

2 cups sprouted cress

1 handful of ripe heirloom mixed cherry or grape tomatoes

1 ripe avocado

1 lime

1 tbsp extra virgin olive oil

Jerk pork

1 lb pork tenderloin

1 tsp ground coriander

olive oil

4 scallions

1 bunch of fresh cilantro

2 cloves garlic

1 thumb-sized piece of gingerroot

1 heaping tbsp honey

½ Scotch bonnet chile (or milder, if you prefer)

2 fresh bay leaves

1 tsp allspice

1 tbsp reduced-sodium soy sauce

2 tbsp red wine vinegar

6 ripe medium tomatoes

To serve

¼ cup fat-free plain yogurt

START COOKING

Put the corn on the grill pan, turning when charred • Arrange the tortillas around a large heatproof bowl and put into the oven to crisp up for 6 minutes • Cut the pork into 8 medallions, flatten them slightly with your fist, then rub with salt, pepper and the ground coriander, and put into the frying pan with 1 tablespoon of olive oil, turning regularly until golden and cooked through

Put the trimmed scallions, most of the fresh cilantro, the peeled garlic and ginger and the rest of the jerk pork ingredients into the blender with a splash of water and whiz until smooth • Remove the pork from the pan, pour in the jerk sauce and let it boil, then return the pork to the pan and reduce to a simmer • Trim the lettuce and break the leaves apart, then arrange them in the tortilla bowl • Carefully hold the charred corn steady and run a knife down the sides to cut off the kernels, then add them to the bowl

Snip the sprouted cress into the bowl, roughly chop and add the tomatoes and peeled, pitted avocado, then gently mix together • Squeeze over the lime juice, add the extra virgin olive oil and a pinch of salt and pepper • Serve the pork and sauce scattered with the remaining cilantro leaves and dollops of yogurt, with the tortilla salad on the side (the salad is really nice dressed with some of the hot sauce)

PORK MARSALA
PORCINI RICE & SPRING GREENS

SERVES 4 | 574 CALORIES

Ingredients out • Kettle boiled • Medium lidded casserole pan or Dutch oven, medium heat • Large frying pan, high heat • Medium lidded saucepan, medium heat

Rice

1 mug (10 oz) of 10-minute
  wholegrain brown or basmati rice
1 big pinch of dried porcini
  mushrooms
½ lemon
a few sprigs of fresh lemon thyme

Pork

1 lb pork tenderloin
1 heaping tsp ground coriander
1 heaping tsp sweet paprika
olive oil
1 small red onion
a few sprigs of fresh sage
1 swig of Marsala
⅓ cup heavy cream, plus
  extra to serve

Greens

1 small head of Savoy cabbage
1 chicken bouillon cube
3 ½ oz Swiss chard or any other
  dark spring greens
½ lemon
1 tbsp extra virgin olive oil

START COOKING

Put 1 mug of rice and 2 mugs of boiling water into the casserole pan, tear in the porcini, add a pinch of salt, the lemon half and lemon thyme, then put the lid on • Refill and boil the kettle • Score lengthways halfway through the center of the pork, open it out like a book, then flatten it slightly with your fist • Rub with salt, pepper, the ground coriander and paprika then put it into the frying pan with 1 tablespoon of olive oil, turning regularly until golden and cooked through

Break off and trim the outer leaves of the cabbage, then roll them up like a cigar and finely slice them • Cut the inner cabbage into thin wedges, then add all of the cabbage to the medium lidded saucepan, crumble in the bouillon cube and cover with boiling water • Finely chop the peeled red onion, pick the sage leaves, then add both to the pork to fry for a few minutes • Add the Swiss chard to the cabbage pan and cover • Once the pork is cooked through, add a good swig of Marsala, carefully light it with a match (if you want) and let the flames subside

Transfer the pork to a board, then pour the heavy cream into the pan and add a ladle or two of broth from the greens, boil and reduce to a nice consistency • Squeeze the juice from the remaining lemon half over the greens, drizzle with the extra virgin olive oil and stir well • Fluff up the rice, carve the pork into ½-inch slices, spoon over the sauce and serve with the greens on the side • Drizzle 1 teaspoon of cream over the pork to finish, if you like

LAMB

LAMB LOLLIPOPS
CURRY SAUCE, RICE & PEAS

SERVES 4 | 632 CALORIES

Ingredients out • Kettle boiled • Medium lidded saucepan, high heat
• Two large non-stick frying pans, medium-high heat

Rice & peas

1 mug (10 oz) of 10-minute
    wholegrain brown or basmati rice
8 whole cloves
1½ oz dried red split lentils
10 oz podded fresh or garden
    peas

Lamb

8 large lamb rib chops on the bone,
    trimmed of fat
1 tbsp garam masala
olive oil
4 scallions
1 fresh red chile
1 thumb-sized piece of gingerroot
4 roasted red peppers (from a jar)
1 heaping tsp honey
balsamic vinegar
3 sprigs of fresh cilantro

Curry sauce

2 tbsp Patak's korma (mild) paste
1 x 14-oz can of light coconut milk
1 lemon

Garnishes

2 uncooked pappadams
fat-free plain yogurt

START COOKING

Put 1 mug of rice and 2 mugs of boiling water into the medium saucepan with a pinch of salt and the cloves, then put the lid on, stirring occasionally • Rub the lamb with salt, pepper and the garam masala, bash and flatten them with your fist, then put into one of the hot frying pans with 1 tablespoon of oil, turning when gnarly and golden brown

Put the korma paste and coconut milk into the other frying pan with the juice of ½ a lemon, stir together, bring to a boil and simmer for 5 minutes, then turn the heat off • Mix the lentils into the rice • Trim and slice the scallions, chile, peeled ginger and peppers, then toss in with the lamb • Stir the peas into the rice and lentils

Pour half the curry sauce into a bowl (pop the rest in the fridge to use another day) • Break up the uncooked pappadams and pop in the microwave (on high) for a minute or two to puff up • At the last minute, toss the lamb with the honey and a splash of balsamic • Serve the lamb scattered with cilantro leaves and scrunched-up pappadams, with the rice and peas, yogurt and lemon wedges on the side

LAMB MEATBALLS
CHOP SALAD & HARISSA YOGURT

Ingredients out • Kettle boiled • Large frying pan, medium heat • Large lidded saucepan, medium-high heat

Meatballs
14 oz ground lamb
1 heaping tsp garam masala
olive oil
1 pinch of saffron
½–1 fresh red chile
2 scallions
½ bunch of fresh cilantro
2 cloves garlic
1 x 14-oz can of chickpeas
1½ cups passata

Salad
½ English cucumber
2 little gem lettuces or hearts of
    romaine
1 bunch of radishes
2 ripe tomatoes
1 tbsp extra virgin olive oil
1 lemon

To serve
1 heaping tsp harissa
⅓ cup fat-free plain yogurt
8 small wholewheat tortillas
1 orange

START COOKING

Mix the ground lamb in a bowl with salt, pepper and the garam masala • Divide into 4, then roll each piece into 4 balls with wet hands, placing them in the frying pan as you roll them and adding 1 tablespoon of olive oil • Toss regularly until dark golden all over • Put the saffron into a cup, just cover with boiling water and leave to soak

Finely slice the chile, trimmed scallions and cilantro stalks (reserving the leaves), put them into the large saucepan with 1 tablespoon of olive oil, then squash in the unpeeled garlic through a garlic press • Fry for 40 seconds, then add the saffron and its soaking water, the drained chickpeas and the passata, cover and bring to a boil • In a small dish, swirl the harissa through the yogurt

Roughly chop and mix all the salad veg for the salad on a board • Add the extra virgin olive oil and lemon juice, then season to taste • Loosen the sauce with a splash of water if needed, then pour into the meatball pan and season to taste • Microwave the tortillas on high for 45 seconds or until warm • Serve it all with orange wedges and a scattering of cilantro leaves

GLAZED SIZZLING CHOPS
SWEET TOMATO & ASPARAGUS LASAGNETTI

Ingredients out • Kettle boiled • Large frying pan, high heat
• Large casserole pan or Dutch oven, medium heat

Lamb

8 large lamb chops, trimmed of fat
olive oil
a few sprigs of fresh rosemary
1 tbsp honey
2 tbsp balsamic vinegar,
   plus extra to serve

Lasagnetti

4 scallions
2 bunches of asparagus (1¼ lbs)
1 fresh red chile
1 pint ripe cherry or grape tomatoes
1 bunch of fresh mint
1 small head of garlic
10 oz fresh lasagne sheets
1 oz Parmesan cheese

START COOKING

Toss the lamb chops with a pinch of salt and put into the frying pan with 1 tablespoon of oil, turning regularly until golden (around 8 minutes) • Trim and finely slice the scallions, asparagus (leaving the tips whole) and chile, and halve the tomatoes • Scrape the veg into the casserole pan with 2 tablespoons of oil

Roughly chop most of the top leafy half of the mint and add to the veg with a pinch of salt and pepper, then squash in 3 cloves of unpeeled garlic through a garlic press • Bash the remaining unpeeled garlic cloves and add to the lamb with the rosemary leaves • Cut the lasagne sheets into ¾-inch-thick strips, scatter them over the veg, then cover with 2 cups of boiling water and mix together

Reduce the heat under the lamb to low and toss with the honey and balsamic to glaze, then remove to a plate to rest • Finely grate the Parmesan over the lasagnetti and turn the heat off • Serve with the lamb, adding an extra drizzle of balsamic and sprinkling over the remaining mint

LAMB KOFTE
PITA & GREEK SALAD

SERVES 4 | 587 CALORIES

*Ingredients out • Kettle boiled • Large frying pan, high heat
• Food processor (metal blade)*

Kofte
14 oz ground lamb
1 tsp garam masala
olive oil
1 oz unsalted raw pistachios
a few sprigs of fresh thyme
1 tbsp honey

Couscous
½ bunch of fresh mint
1 fresh red chile
½ mug (5 oz) of couscous

Salad
½ head of iceberg lettuce
½ red onion
½ English cucumber
5 ripe cherry or grape tomatoes
4 black olives (with pits)
⅓ cup fat-free plain yogurt
2 lemons
1½ oz feta cheese

To serve
4 pita breads

START COOKING

In a large bowl, mix the ground lamb with salt, pepper and the garam masala • Divide into 8, then with wet hands shape into little fat fingers • Put into the frying pan with 1 tablespoon of oil, turning until dark golden all over • Tear off most of the top leafy half of the mint and blitz in the processor with a pinch of salt and pepper and the chile until fine • Remove the blade, stir in ½ a mug of couscous and 1 mug of boiling water, put the lid on and leave to sit in the processor

Cut the lettuce into wedges and arrange on a nice board or platter • Peel and coarsely grate the onion and cucumber into a bowl, season well with salt, then squeeze out any excess salty liquid and sprinkle over the lettuce • Chop and add the tomatoes, then squash, pit and dot over the olives • Mix the yogurt in a bowl with the juice of 1 lemon, season to taste, then drizzle it over the lettuce and crumble over the feta

Bash the pistachios in a pestle and mortar • Drain away the fat from the lamb, then toss with the bashed nuts, thyme leaves and honey, and turn the heat off • Pop the pitas in the microwave on high for 45 seconds to warm through, then cut in half and add to the board with the kofte • Fluff up the couscous, scatter the remaining mint leaves over everything and serve with lemon wedges

QUICK LAMB TAGINE
PAN-FRIED EGGPLANT & CUMIN CRUNCH

Ingredients out • Kettle boiled • Large frying pan, high heat • Medium frying pan, medium heat

Lamb & eggplant
2 small eggplants
10 oz boneless lamb leg steak
 (cut ½-inch thick)
1 heaping tsp garam masala
olive oil
a few sprigs of fresh cilantro

Couscous
1 mug (10 oz) of couscous

Cumin crunch
1 heaping tbsp unsalted raw
 pistachios
1 heaping tbsp raw sesame seeds
1 tbsp cumin seeds

Veg
1 good pinch of saffron
1½ lbs ripe heirloom mixed
 tomatoes
1 preserved lemon
4 scallions
½–1 fresh red chile

To serve
¼ cup fat-free plain yogurt

START COOKING

Cook the eggplants whole in the microwave on high for 7 minutes • Put 1 mug of couscous and 2 mugs of boiling water into a bowl and cover • Cut the lamb into 8 pieces and flatten with your fist, then toss with salt, pepper and the garam masala • Put into the large frying pan with 1 tablespoon of oil, turning when golden • Toast the cumin crunch mix in the medium frying pan until lightly golden, then pound in a pestle and mortar • Return the empty pan to a low heat

Carefully transfer the eggplants to a board, then halve lengthways and add to the lamb pan, skin-side down, pushing the lamb to the side • Put the saffron into a mug half-filled with boiling water • Roughly chop the tomatoes, finely chop the preserved lemon, trim and slice the scallions and chile, then add it all to the medium frying pan with 2 tablespoons of oil and the saffron and its soaking water • Turn the heat up to high, bring to a boil, then season to taste

Fluff up the couscous, then spoon over a large serving board or platter • Flip the eggplant over to soak up the pan juices, then place on top of the couscous and pour over the tomatoes and any juices • Lay over the lamb, then scatter with the cumin crunch and the cilantro leaves • Serve with the yogurt

MUSTARD LAMB
IRISH MASH & WATERCRESS APPLE SALAD

SERVES 4 | 538 CALORIES

Mash

3 leeks
1½ lbs potatoes
reduced-fat (2%) milk
1 whole nutmeg, for grating
optional: 2 tbsp unsalted butter

Lamb

14 oz boneless lamb leg steak
   (cut ½-inch thick)
2 tsp dry mustard powder
canola oil
1 heaping tbsp all-purpose flour
1 cup quality hard cider
2 heaping tsp mint sauce

Salad

1 inner celery heart
1 eating apple
4 cups watercress
1 bunch of fresh mint
1 tbsp cider vinegar

Ingredients out • Kettle boiled • Food processor (thick slicer & coarse grater) • Medium lidded saucepan, high heat • Large frying pan, high heat

START COOKING

Split the leeks lengthways, rinse under the cold tap, then thickly slice with the potatoes in the processor, put into the medium saucepan with a pinch of salt, cover with boiling water and the lid and boil hard until tender, then drain – keep an eye on it • Score lengthways halfway through the center of each piece of lamb and open out like a book • Sprinkle with salt, pepper and the mustard powder, then put into the frying pan with 1 tablespoon of oil, turning when golden

Swap to the coarse grater on your processor, pick and reserve any yellow celery leaves, then coarsely grate the stalks in the processor with the apple • Tip onto a platter with the watercress • Roughly chop and add the top leafy half of the mint • Drizzle with cider vinegar and 1 tablespoon of oil, season to taste and toss

Mash the drained potatoes and leeks, season well to taste, then loosen to your liking with a splash of milk, add a few scrapings of nutmeg and the butter, if using, and spoon onto a large platter • Transfer the lamb to a plate, then stir the flour into the lamb pan, followed by the cider • Pour in any lamb resting juices, then stir in the mint sauce and bring to a boil • Slice up the lamb and serve with the mash and gravy, scattered with the reserved celery leaves, and the salad on the side

TURKISH FLATS
SHRED SALAD, FETA & HERBS

SERVES 4 | 525 CALORIES

Ingredients out • Oven at full whack (475°F)
• Large frying pan, high heat • Food processor (fine slicer)

Flats

olive oil

8 oz lean ground lamb

1 tsp cumin seeds

1 tsp sweet smoked paprika

2 oz raw walnut halves

2 sprigs of fresh rosemary

2 cloves garlic

2 tbsp tomato paste

1 lemon

4 large flour tortillas

Salad

4 scallions

1 green bell pepper

¼ English cucumber

3 ripe tomatoes

1 little gem lettuce or heart of
romaine

½ bunch of fresh cilantro

½ bunch of fresh dill

1 tbsp extra virgin olive oil

1 tbsp red wine vinegar

1 oz feta cheese

To serve

4 heaping tsp low-fat hummus

optional: hot chili sauce

optional: pickled chiles

START COOKING

Put 1 tablespoon of olive oil into the frying pan with the ground lamb, salt, pepper, cumin seeds and paprika • Crumble in the walnuts, strip in the rosemary leaves and break everything apart with a wooden spoon, stirring regularly until golden • Trim the scallions, tear the stalks and seeds out of the pepper, then slice all the salad veg and herb leaves in the processor, tip onto a serving platter

Squash the unpeeled garlic through a garlic press into the lamb pan • Stir in the tomato paste and lemon juice, then take the pan off the heat • Lay the tortillas over 2 large baking sheets and spread the lamb mixture evenly across them with the back of a spoon • Pop into the oven for 5 minutes to crisp up

Dress the salad veg with the extra virgin olive oil and vinegar, toss together, then season to taste and crumble over the feta • Top and stuff the tortillas with loads of salad, then serve with hummus, and chili sauce or pickled chiles, if you like

FISH

ASIAN SEA BASS
STICKY RICE & DRESSED GREENS

SERVES 4 | 629 CALORIES

Ingredients out • *Kettle boiled* • *Medium lidded saucepan, medium heat*
• *Casserole pan or Dutch oven, medium heat* • *Food processor (metal blade)*

Fish

4 small whole sea bass
(roughly 10 oz each), gutted and
scaled
1 thumb-sized piece of gingerroot
2 cloves garlic
1 lemongrass stalk
1 bunch of fresh cilantro
1 fresh red chile
2 scallions
3 tbsp reduced-sodium soy sauce,
plus extra to serve
1 tbsp fish sauce
Asian sesame oil
2 limes

Rice

1 x 14-oz can of light coconut milk
1 coconut milk can or 1 cup
basmati rice

Greens

1 bunch of asparagus (10 oz)
2 bok choy
7 oz sugar snap peas
1 lime

START COOKING

Score the fish 5 times on each side down to the bone, then season all over and lay in a snug-fitting, high-sided pan • Pour in 1½ cups of boiling water, cover tightly with a double layer of aluminum foil and place on a medium-high heat to steam • Pour the coconut milk, 1 can's worth of rice and 1 can of boiling water (use a tea towel to hold the can) into the medium saucepan • Add a pinch of salt, stir well, cover and cook for roughly 10 minutes, stirring occasionally, then turn the heat off • Pour the rest of the boiling water into the casserole pan

Peel the ginger, garlic and the outer leaves of the lemongrass, roughly chop them and put into the processor • Add the cilantro stalks (reserving the leaves), chile, trimmed scallions, soy and fish sauces, 1 teaspoon of oil and the juice of 2 limes to the processor and pulse until finely chopped, then pour into a bowl

Trim the asparagus, halve the bok choy and add both to the boiling water in the casserole pan with the sugar snaps • Cook for 2 minutes, then drain and toss with 1 tablespoon of oil and the juice of 1 lime, season to taste with soy sauce and serve with the fluffed-up rice • Uncover the fish, spoon some of its juices into the dressing, then pour everything back over the fish and serve scattered with cilantro leaves

GRILLED CAJUN SHRIMP
SWEET POTATO MASH & HOLY TRINITY VEG

SERVES 4 | 396 CALORIES

Ingredients out • *Kettle boiled* • *Oven broiler on high* • *Food processor (thick slicer)*
• *Large lidded saucepan, high heat* • *Large frying pan, medium heat*

Mash
1½ lbs sweet potatoes
1½ oz Cheddar cheese

Shrimp
16 jumbo raw shell-on tiger shrimp
3 cloves garlic
1 heaping tbsp Cajun seasoning
olive oil
½ bunch of fresh thyme
1 lemon

Veg
1 green bell pepper
1 red bell pepper
2 celery stalks
5 scallions
½ fresh red chile
1 big handful of frozen corn
1 tsp sweet smoked paprika

START COOKING

Wash the sweet potatoes and slice in the processor • Put into the lidded saucepan with a pinch of salt, then cover with boiling water and the lid • Put the shrimp into a roasting pan, squash over the unpeeled garlic through a garlic press, then toss with the Cajun seasoning, 1 tablespoon of oil and the thyme sprigs • Spread out in a single layer and pop on a high heat for a couple of minutes to crisp the bottoms of the shrimp up, then place under the broiler until the tops are sizzling, golden and crispy

Seed and roughly chop the peppers and put into the frying pan with 1 tablespoon of oil • Trim and slice the celery, scallions and chile, and add to the pan along with the corn and paprika • Season with salt and pepper and keep things moving

When cooked through, drain the sweet potatoes in a colander • Return to the pan and mash well • Grate in the cheese, mix well and season to taste • Scatter the veg over the mash and serve with the crispy shrimp and lemon wedges

CRACKIN' CRAB BRIKS
COUSCOUS SALAD & SALSA

SERVES 4 | 457 CALORIES

Ingredients out • *Kettle boiled* • *Large frying pan, medium heat*
• *Food processor (coarse grater)*

Briks
1–2 preserved lemons
2 scallions
½ bunch of fresh cilantro
14 oz crabmeat (a mixture
   of brown and white meat)
2 tsp harissa, plus extra to serve
4 large sheets of phyllo pastry
   olive oil

Salad
½ tsp caraway seeds
½ mug (5 oz) of couscous
2 tsp sun-dried tomato paste
½ bulb fennel
½ bunch of fresh mint
1 lemon
extra virgin olive oil
1 pomegranate

Salsa
1 large ripe tomato
1 thumb-sized piece of gingerroot
½ lemon

To serve
fat-free plain yogurt

START COOKING

Finely chop the preserved lemons, trimmed scallions and cilantro (stalks and all) • Mix in a bowl with the crabmeat and harissa • Lay out a sheet of phyllo pastry, add ¼ of the mixture and shape into the size of a deck of playing cards at the center of the bottom of the sheet, then push your thumb into the center of the filling to make a space for it to expand as it cooks • Fold in the sides, then fold them up • Repeat until you have 4 briks • Put 1 tablespoon of olive oil into the pan, then add the briks and cook until golden and crisp on both sides • Add the caraway seeds to the side of the pan and toast for a minute, then scrape into a salad bowl

Put ½ a mug of couscous, 1 mug of boiling water, the tomato paste and a pinch of salt into a bowl and cover • Pick and reserve the fennel tops, then roughly chop and grate the bulb in the processor • Tip into the salad bowl, then chop and add the top leafy half of the mint • Squeeze in the lemon juice and drizzle with 1 tablespoon of extra virgin olive oil • Season to taste and toss everything together

Finely grate the tomato and ginger into a little bowl • Add a pinch of salt and pepper, a good squeeze of lemon juice and 1 tablespoon of extra virgin olive oil and mix together • Fluff up the couscous, then tip onto a platter • Pile the salad in the middle, then bash the halved pomegranate over the top so the seeds tumble out • Scatter over the reserved fennel tops, pop the crab briks on a board and serve with dollops of yogurt and the salsa

MIXED FISH GRILL
MEDITERRANEAN FENNEL & COUSCOUS

Ingredients out • *Kettle boiled* • *Oven at full whack (475°F)*
• *Large lidded saucepan, low heat* • *Food processor (fine slicer)*

Fish
1 bunch of fresh Italian parsley
1 fresh red chile
12 ripe heirloom mixed cherry
   or grape tomatoes
2 cloves garlic
olive oil
½ lemon
14 oz mixed fish fillets (striped bass
   or trout), scaled and pin-boned
4 jumbo raw shell-on shrimp
1 lb clams and mussels, scrubbed
   clean and debearded

Couscous
1 mug (10 oz) of couscous

Fennel
4 sun-dried tomatoes packed in oil
   (from a jar)
1 sprig of fresh rosemary
1 handful of mixed olives (with pits)
2 bulbs fennel
1 lemon

To serve
1 lemon
¼ cup fat-free plain yogurt

START COOKING

Roughly chop the parsley leaves and chile, and put into a large, high-sided roasting pan with the tomatoes • Squash in the unpeeled garlic through a garlic press and mix with 1 tablespoon of oil, salt, pepper and the juice of ½ a lemon • Halve the fish fillets, then add to the pan with the shellfish (throw away any mussels or clams that won't close when tapped), and toss together • Cook in the oven for 10 minutes, or until the clams and mussels have opened (throw away any that remain closed)

Put 1 mug of couscous, 2 mugs of boiling water and a pinch of salt and pepper into a bowl, then cover • Put the sun-dried tomatoes and a splash of their oil, the rosemary leaves and olives into the large saucepan • Halve the fennel bulbs, then finely slice in the processor, and add to the pan with a pinch of salt and the juice of 1 lemon • Turn the heat up to high and cover with the lid, stirring regularly

Fluff up the couscous • Season the fennel to taste • Serve with the pan of fish, lemon wedges and the yogurt for dolloping over

ASIAN FISH
MISO NOODLES & CRUNCHY VEG

Ingredients out • Kettle boiled • Oven at 400°F
• Casserole pan or Dutch oven, high heat • Food processor (fine slicer)

Fish

2 tsp Asian sesame oil

10 oz salmon fillet, skin off
  and pin-boned

10 oz any white fish fillet,
  skin off and pin-boned

1 tbsp raw sesame seeds

1 lime

1 tbsp honey

2 sprigs of fresh cilantro

Noodles

1 tbsp white miso paste

2 tbsp reduced-sodium soy sauce,
  plus extra to serve

5 dried kaffir lime leaves

3 nests of fine egg noodles

1 fresh red chile

½ English cucumber

7 oz sugar snap peas

4 scallions

1 little gem lettuce or heart of
  romaine

7 oz radishes

1 lime

2 tbsp extra virgin olive oil

START COOKING

Rub half the sesame oil on a small shallow baking dish or ovenproof serving platter • Pat both fish dry with paper towel, slice them into ½-inch-thick strips and arrange randomly around the dish or platter • Rub gently with the rest of the sesame oil and season with salt and pepper • Scatter over the sesame seeds, finely grate over the zest from 1 lime and squeeze over half the juice, then drizzle over the honey • Place in the oven to cook through (roughly 7 minutes)

Pour 4 cups of boiling water into the casserole pan with the miso paste, soy sauce, crumbled lime leaves and noodles, making sure they're fully submerged • Slice the chile and add to the broth • Finely slice the cucumber, sugar snaps, trimmed scallions, lettuce and radishes in the processor

Tip the sliced veg into a bowl and dress with the juice of 1 lime, a little soy sauce and the extra virgin olive oil • Check the noodles and switch off the heat when they're done, then season the broth to taste with soy sauce • Pile the veg in the center of the noodles and toss together at the table • Serve the fish sprinkled with cilantro leaves

SHRIMP COCKTAIL
JUMBO SHRIMP & SUN-DRIED PAN BREAD

Ingredients out • Food processor (metal blade) • 11-inch frying pan, medium heat • Medium frying pan, medium heat

Bread

1⅓ cups self-rising flour, plus extra
  for dusting
3 ½ oz sun-dried tomatoes packed
  in oil (from a jar)
3 sprigs of fresh basil
olive oil

Shrimp cocktail

1 handful of mixed seeds
3 scallions
1 head of romaine lettuce
½ English cucumber
3 ripe heirloom mixed tomatoes
1 ripe avocado
1 cup sprouted cress
14 oz small cooked peeled shrimp
⅓ cup fat-free plain yogurt
1 tsp Worcestershire sauce
1 tsp Tabasco
1 heaping tbsp tomato ketchup
1 tbsp brandy
1 lemon
1 tsp extra virgin olive oil

Jumbo shrimp

1 good pinch of cayenne pepper
4 jumbo raw shell-on shrimp
4 cloves garlic

START COOKING

Blitz the flour, sun-dried tomatoes (drained) and basil in the processor, then gradually add small splashes of water to form a ball of dough • On a flour-dusted surface, shape the dough into an 11-inch round • Put 1 tablespoon of olive oil and the dough into the 11-inch pan, pat it out to the edges and cook until nicely golden, turning halfway (roughly 5 minutes on each side) • Put the seeds in the medium pan to toast, tossing often

Randomly slice up the trimmed scallions, lettuce, cucumber and tomatoes on a nice serving board • Squeeze and squidge over the avocado flesh, discarding the skin and pit, and snip over the cress • Place the small shrimp in the middle of the salad and pile the toasted seeds to one side, returning the pan to the heat • Add 1 tablespoon of olive oil to the medium pan with the cayenne pepper and jumbo shrimp, then squash in the unpeeled garlic through a garlic press, and fry, turning regularly until golden

In a bowl, mix the yogurt with the Worcestershire sauce, Tabasco, ketchup, brandy and the juice from ½ a lemon, then season to taste • Spoon the sauce over the shrimp • When the jumbo shrimp are crispy, place on the board • Drizzle with a little extra virgin olive oil and lemon juice from a height and serve with torn-up pieces of the incredible pan bread

SMOKED SALMON
YORKSHIRE PUD, BEETS & ASPARAGUS

SERVES 4 | 407 CALORIES

Yorkshire pud
olive oil
2–3 sprigs of fresh rosemary
2 large eggs
⅔ cup reduced-fat (2%) milk
½ cup all-purpose flour
6 oz quality smoked salmon

Beets & asparagus
1 bunch of asparagus (10 oz)
8 oz cooked beets
¼ cup balsamic vinegar
1 heaping tsp honey
2 cups sprouted cress
2 sprigs of fresh basil
½ lemon

Dressing
3 heaping tbsp fat-free plain
  yogurt
2 heaping tbsp grated
  horseradish (from a jar)
1 lemon

Ingredients out • Oven at 400°F
• 11-inch non-stick ovenproof frying pan, high heat • Blender
• Grill pan, high heat • Casserole pan or Dutch oven, medium heat

START COOKING
Put 2 tablespoons of oil into the frying pan and pick in the rosemary leaves
• Crack the eggs into the blender, add the milk and flour, then blitz until
smooth • Spread out the rosemary in the pan, then pour in the batter, let it
fry for 30 seconds, then pop into the oven and close the door until golden
(roughly 13 minutes) • Trim the asparagus and put dry on the hot grill pan,
turning until nicely charred on all sides

Drain and slice or dice the beets, then place in the casserole pan with the
balsamic and honey, stirring regularly, and removing from the heat when
sticky • Mix the yogurt and horseradish in a bowl, then season to taste with
salt, pepper and lemon juice • Snip the sprouted cress onto a nice serving
board, and spoon the beets on top, then pick over the basil leaves

Shake the asparagus with a squeeze of lemon juice, salt and pepper, and
immediately pile on the board • Wait by the oven until your Yorkshire
pudding is puffed up and beautiful • Once it looks so good you can't stand
it any longer, get it out of the oven, slide it onto the board, then roll the
smoked salmon into roses and place on top • Serve straight away with
lemon wedges on the side

GRILLED TUNA
KINDA NIÇOISE SALAD

SERVES 4 | 491 CALORIES

Ingredients out • Kettle boiled • Medium lidded saucepan, high heat • Grill pan, high heat • Blender

Salad

12 oz mixed green and
   yellow beans
½ a baguette
12 black olives (with pits)
3 ripe heirloom mixed tomatoes
1 head of romaine lettuce
¾ oz feta cheese
1 lemon

Tuna & dressings

1 big bunch of fresh basil
6 anchovy fillets
1 lemon
¼ cup extra virgin olive oil
2 x 7-oz tuna steaks (1-inch thick)
1 tbsp red wine vinegar
1 heaping tsp grainy mustard
1 tsp honey

START COOKING

Line the beans up and cut off the stalks, put them into the saucepan with a pinch of salt, then cover with boiling water and the lid • Slice the baguette into ¾-inch chunks and put on the grill pan, turning when golden • Pick and reserve 10 baby sprigs of basil • Rip off the rest of the leaves and blitz them in the blender with the anchovies, juice of 1 lemon, the extra virgin olive oil and a splash of water

Pour about 40% of the dressing onto a nice serving platter and put aside • Rub 10% into the tuna and season with salt and pepper • Pour the rest of the dressing into a big bowl with the vinegar, mustard and honey, then mix together • Drain the cooked beans, remove the pits from the olives, roughly chop the tomatoes, then add it all to the bowl of dressing and toss together

Put the tuna on the grill pan and cook for 2 minutes on each side, or until blushing in the middle • Chop the lettuce into ¾-inch chunks, tear the toasts into croutons and arrange over a large board with the lettuce • Scatter the dressed beans, olives and tomatoes over the top • Tear each tuna steak in half and add to the dressing platter • Scatter over the reserved basil leaves, crumble over the feta and serve with lemon wedges

STICKY SQUID BALLS
GRILLED SHRIMP & NOODLE BROTH

SERVES 4 | 489 CALORIES

*Ingredients out • Kettle boiled • Large lidded saucepan, high heat
• Food processor (fine slicer & metal blade) • Large frying pan, medium heat*

Broth

2 chicken bouillon cubes

14 oz sugar snap peas

½ head of Napa cabbage

2 fresh red chiles

1 bunch of broccolini (7 oz)

2 bok choy

1 bunch of radishes

1 thumb-sized piece of gingerroot

1 tbsp fish sauce

2 tbsp reduced-sodium soy sauce

4 nests of egg noodles

2 limes

Squid & shrimp

8 oz fresh squid, gutted
  and cleaned

½ bunch of fresh cilantro

1 tbsp Asian sesame oil

8 oz large raw peeled tiger shrimp

sweet red chili sauce

1 tbsp raw sesame seeds

START COOKING

Pour 6 cups of boiling water into the large saucepan and crumble in the bouillon cubes • Slice the sugar snaps, cabbage and 1 chile in the processor, then tip into a large bowl • Trim the ends off the broccolini, quarter the bok choy and add both to the bowl, along with the radishes • Finely grate half the peeled ginger and finely slice half a chile, then add both to the broth with the fish and soy sauces, and cover with a lid

Swap to the metal blade, add the remaining chile and ginger, the squid (pat dry with paper towel first), cilantro stalks, salt and pepper, then blitz to a paste, using a spatula to scrape the mixture from the sides after a minute • Put the sesame oil into the frying pan • Use 2 dessert spoons to scrape and dollop the squid around the pan so you get 8 balls • Fry, turning when nicely golden, and adding the shrimp after turning

Stir the noodles and veg into the broth, pop the lid back on and bring back to a boil • Turn the shrimp, drizzle over some sweet chili sauce, scatter over the sesame seeds, then gently shake the pan to coat • Squeeze the limes into the broth, stir and season to perfection • Ladle the noodles, veg and broth into bowls and serve the seafood on top • Finish with the cilantro leaves

MOROCCAN BASS
COUSCOUS, POMEGRANATE & HARISSA

Ingredients out • Kettle boiled • Large frying pan, medium-high heat • Food processor (metal blade)

SERVES 4 | 611 CALORIES

Fish

4 x 10-oz whole striped bass,
  heads and tails removed,
  scaled and gutted
olive oil
1 big pinch of saffron
4 scallions
a few sprigs of fresh thyme
1 tsp harissa, plus extra to serve

Couscous & salsa

1 mug (10 oz) of couscous
1 preserved lemon
2 ½ oz soft dried apricots
6 roasted red peppers (from a jar)
1 bunch of fresh cilantro
1 pomegranate

To serve

2 tbsp unsalted raw pistachios
1 tbsp raw sesame seeds
⅓ cup fat-free plain yogurt
1 tsp rose water

START COOKING

Toast the pistachios and sesame seeds in the pan for 1 minute, then remove and place the pan back on the heat • Score the fish in a crisscross fashion on both sides down to the bone • Season all over with salt and pepper and add to the pan with 1 tablespoon of oil, then cook for 3 minutes on each side • Put 1 mug of couscous, 2 mugs of boiling water and a pinch of salt into a bowl and cover • Cover the saffron with ⅔ cup boiling water

Blitz the preserved lemon, apricots, peppers and half the cilantro in the processor until fine, then spoon into a bowl, squeeze in the juice of ½ the pomegranate, mix, season to taste and put aside • Slice the trimmed scallions and add to the fish with the thyme sprigs, harissa, saffron and soaking water • Scrunch up and wet a sheet of parchment paper and tuck it over the fish

Spoon the yogurt into a small bowl, then swirl through the rose water and a little harissa • Fluff up the couscous, tip it over a warm platter or board and spoon over the salsa • Lay the fish on top, spoon over some of the juices, then scatter over the toasted nuts and seeds • Hold the second pomegranate half in the palm of your hand and bash the back of it with a spoon so the seeds tumble over the salad • Finish with the rest of the cilantro leaves

GREEN TEA SALMON
COCONUT RICE & MISO GREENS

SERVES 4 | 603 CALORIES

Ingredients out • *Kettle boiled* • *Large frying pan, medium-high heat* • *Large lidded saucepan, medium heat* • *Medium lidded saucepan, medium heat* • *Blender*

Salmon

4 x 4-oz salmon fillets, skin on, scaled and pin-boned
2 green tea bags
olive oil

Rice

1 x 14-oz can of light coconut milk
1 coconut milk can or 1 cup basmati rice
½ lemon

Greens

½–1 fresh red chile
1 small thumb-sized piece of gingerroot
1 heaping tsp white miso powder or 1 tbsp white miso paste
½ bunch of fresh cilantro
½ lemon
2–3 tbsp reduced-sodium soy sauce
1 heaping tsp honey
7 oz sugar snap peas
1 bunch of broccolini (7 oz)
1 bunch of asparagus (10 oz)
1 lime

START COOKING

Put the salmon on a plate, rip open the green tea bags and scatter the contents over the fish, season with salt and pepper and rub in • Put into the frying pan, skin-side down, with 1 teaspoon of oil, turning until golden on all sides • Pour the coconut milk, 1 can's worth of rice and 1 can of boiling water (use a tea towel to hold the can) into the large saucepan • Add ½ a lemon, stir well, cover and cook for roughly 10 minutes, stirring occasionally, then turn the heat off

Finely slice ½ the chile for garnish and throw the rest into the blender with the peeled ginger, the miso powder or paste, most of the cilantro, the juice of ½ a lemon, the soy sauce, honey and a splash of water, then whiz until smooth • Pour the rest of the boiled water into the medium saucepan • Add the sugar snaps, trimmed broccolini and asparagus and a pinch of salt and cook for a few minutes, until just tender

Remove the cooked salmon from the pan, gently pull the skins off and put back soft-side down to crisp up for 30 seconds • Pour the dressing onto a platter, then quickly drain the greens and place nicely on top • Fluff up the rice, then flake the salmon over the top, sprinkle with the chile and the rest of the cilantro leaves, then serve with the crispy salmon skin and lime wedges

ARNOLD BENNETT FRITTATA
FOCACCIA & EMMENTAL WALDORF SALAD

Ingredients out • *Kettle boiled* • *Oven broiler on high* • *Large casserole pan or Dutch oven, high heat* • *10-inch non-stick ovenproof frying pan, medium heat*

Frittata

8 oz undyed smoked haddock
4 fresh bay leaves
8 large eggs
6 scallions
½ bunch of fresh mint
1 large handful of frozen peas
olive oil
½ oz Parmesan cheese

Salad

2 eating apples
1 lemon
½ bunch of fresh chives
1 handful of raw walnut halves
3 cups watercress
2 tbsp extra virgin olive oil
1 oz Emmental cheese

To serve

7 oz focaccia bread
1 lemon

START COOKING

Put the fish and bay leaves into the casserole pan and cover with boiling water • Pop the focaccia on the very bottom shelf of the broiler to toast • Beat the eggs in a large bowl with a pinch of salt and pepper • Trim and finely slice the scallions and the top leafy part of the mint and mix into the eggs, along with the peas

Use a slotted spatula to remove the fish to a bowl, then flake with a fork, discarding the skin • Turn the heat under the frying pan up to high, add 1 tablespoon of olive oil and pour in the egg mixture • Stir for a minute until it begins to set • Sprinkle over the poached haddock, finely grate over a dusting of Parmesan then put the pan under the broiler on the top shelf until cooked through, fluffy and golden (roughly 5 minutes)

On a nice large board, matchstick or coarsely grate the apples, then quickly squeeze over some lemon juice to stop them discoloring • Finely chop the chives and sprinkle them over the apple • Crumble over the walnuts, add the watercress and drizzle with the extra virgin olive oil, then toss together and season to taste • Peel slices of Emmental over the top • Get the frittata and focaccia out from under the broiler and serve straight away with lemon wedges

MOROCCAN MUSSELS
TAPENADE TOASTIES & CUCUMBER SALAD

SERVES 4 | 549 CALORIES

Ingredients out • *Large high-sided roasting pan, low heat* • *Blender* • *Large grill pan, high heat*

Mussels

olive oil
3 cloves garlic
2 heaping tsp harissa
2 x 14-oz cans of diced tomatoes
½ bunch of fresh cilantro
2 preserved lemons
1 pinch of saffron
5 lbs mussels, scrubbed clean
  and debearded

To serve

1 ciabatta loaf
1 head of bibb lettuce
½ English cucumber
a few sprigs of fresh mint
½ lemon
¼ cup fat-free plain yogurt
½ clove garlic
1 x 3-oz jar of sun-dried tomato
  tapenade

START COOKING

Pour 2 tablespoons of oil into the roasting pan • Squash in the unpeeled garlic through a garlic press and stir in the harissa • Pour the tomatoes into the blender with most of the cilantro, salt, pepper, the preserved lemons and the saffron, purée, then pour into the pan and turn the heat up

Bring the sauce to a boil, then stir in the mussels (throw away any open ones that don't close when tapped) and cover well with a double layer of aluminum foil, pinching it at the sides to seal (use a tea towel to protect your hands) • Cut the ciabatta lengthways into quarters and put on the grill pan, turning when golden and charred • Cut the lettuce into quarters and place on a big board

Using a box grater, coarsely grate the cucumber in long strokes, add a good pinch of salt, then toss and squeeze to get rid of the excess salty liquid, and pop in a bowl • Rip off the top leafy half of the mint, finely chop it and add to the cucumber with the lemon juice and yogurt, then season to taste and spoon over the lettuce • Rub the toast with ½ a garlic clove and spread over the tapenade • Check to see if the mussels have opened up (throw away any that remain closed), then sprinkle with the remaining cilantro leaves, correct the seasoning of the sauce and serve with the toasties and salad

GOLDEN SCALLOPS
SUN-BLUSH MASH & GREENS

SERVES 4 | 441 CALORIES

Ingredients out • Kettle boiled • Large shallow lidded casserole pan or Dutch oven, high heat • Medium pan, high heat • Food processor (metal blade) • Large frying pan, medium heat

Sun-blush mash

1½ lbs potatoes
1½ oz Cheddar cheese
2 ½ oz sun-dried tomatoes packed in oil (from a jar)
optional: 1 splash of milk

Veg

1 bunch of broccolini (7 oz)
7 oz asparagus spears
7 oz frozen peas
1 tbsp extra virgin olive oil
½ lemon

Scallops

4 rashers of smoked bacon
12 large sea scallops
olive oil
20 fresh sage leaves
½ lemon

START COOKING

Slice the potatoes ½-inch thick, put into the casserole pan with a pinch of salt, then cover with boiling water and the lid • Refill and boil the kettle • Trim the ends off the broccolini and asparagus (I like to put the asparagus through a runner bean cutter, if you've got one, or you can leave them whole) • Put both veg into the medium pan with the peas, cover with boiling water and cook for 3 minutes • Drain, toss with the extra virgin olive oil and the juice of ½ a lemon, and put into a serving bowl

Crumble the cheese into the processor, add the sun-dried tomatoes and ½ a tablespoon of their oil and blitz well • Finely slice the bacon • Pat the scallops dry with paper towel, then score on one side in deep crisscrosses and season with salt and pepper • Put 1 tablespoon of olive oil into the hot frying pan and add the scallops, scored-side down • Cook until lightly golden on both sides, then add the bacon and sage leaves

Drain the potatoes, tip into the processor and pulse up (oozy is good, but over-blitz and the mash will go gluey – not good), loosen with a splash of milk if needed • Check the seasoning and spoon onto a serving platter • Squeeze the juice of ½ a lemon over the scallops, shake and toss the pan, then serve right away with the veg on the side

KILLER KEDGEREE
BEANS, GREENS & CHILI YOGURT

SERVES 4 | 474 CALORIES

Ingredients out • *Kettle boiled* • *Large frying pan, high heat*
• *Large casserole pan or Dutch oven, medium heat* • *Medium lidded*
saucepan, medium heat

Kedgeree

2 large eggs
4 fresh bay leaves
1 lb any undyed smoked white fish
  fillets, scaled and pin-boned
1 thumb-sized piece of gingerroot
1 fresh red chile
1 bunch of scallions
1 bunch of fresh cilantro
2 heaping tsp mustard seeds
2 heaping tsp turmeric
olive oil
2 x 8-oz packages of ready-made
  wholegrain brown rice
10 oz frozen peas
1 lemon

Greens

7 oz fine green beans
1 big bunch of Swiss chard
1 tbsp extra virgin olive oil
½ lemon

Yogurt

3 tbsp fat-free plain yogurt
1 tbsp sweet chili sauce
½ lemon

START COOKING

Fill the frying pan with boiling water, add the eggs, bay leaves and smoked fish, then reduce to a simmer • Refill and boil the kettle • Finely chop or slice the peeled ginger, chile, trimmed scallions and cilantro (reserving a few leaves) • Put the mustard seeds and turmeric into the casserole pan with 1 tablespoon of olive oil, and when they pop, scrape in the chopped veg from the board, stirring regularly

Line the beans up and trim the ends, put into the medium saucepan with a pinch of salt, then cover with boiling water and the lid • Line up your chard leaves, cut off and slice the stalks and add the stalks to the beans • Stir the cooked rice, peas and the juice from 1 lemon into the casserole pan • Add the chard leaves to the beans for a minute • Ripple the yogurt, chili sauce and the juice of ½ a lemon together in a bowl

Drain the greens and leave to steam dry • Use a slotted spatula to remove the smoked fish from the pan, flake it into the rice, discarding the skin, stir and mix up beautifully, then season to taste • Peel the eggs under the cold tap and cut into quarters, place around the kedgeree pan and scatter over the reserved cilantro leaves • Dress the greens on a board with the extra virgin olive oil and lemon juice, then season to taste and serve

MIGHTY MACKEREL
MIXED TOMATO & QUINOA SALAD

SERVES 4 | 431 CALORIES

Salad

1 mug (10 oz) of quinoa
½ lemon
1½ lbs ripe heirloom mixed
    tomatoes
1 fresh red chile
2 tbsp extra virgin olive oil
1 tbsp balsamic vinegar

Mackerel

4 x 7-oz whole mackerel,
    scaled and gutted
1 heaping tsp ground coriander
olive oil
2 sprigs of fresh rosemary
2 cloves garlic

To serve

2 heaping tbsp fat-free plain
    yogurt
2 heaping tsp grated
    horseradish (from a jar)
a couple of sprigs of fresh basil

Ingredients out • Kettle boiled • Medium lidded saucepan, medium heat • Large frying pan, high heat

START COOKING

Put 1 mug of quinoa and 2 mugs of boiling water into the medium saucepan with a pinch of salt and the lemon half, then pop the lid on and stir every now and again • On parchment paper, score the mackerel on both sides at ¾-inch intervals down to the bone • Rub all over with salt, pepper and the ground coriander, then put into the large frying pan with 1 tablespoon of olive oil

Slice the tomatoes any way you like and arrange on a large board or platter, then finely slice and sprinkle over the chile • Strip the rosemary leaves over the fish, then crush and add the whole garlic cloves • Turn the fish when golden (roughly 4 to 5 minutes on each side)

When the quinoa is cooked (after roughly 10 minutes), drain it and use tongs to squeeze over the lemon juice, then spoon the quinoa into the center of the tomatoes • Drizzle with the extra virgin olive oil and balsamic, and a pinch of salt and pepper • Lay the crispy fish on top • Mix the yogurt and horseradish together and dollop it over the fish • Pick over the basil leaves and serve

POACHED FISH
CODDLED EGGS & TOMATO LOAF

SERVES 4 | 633 CALORIES

Ingredients out • *Kettle boiled* • *Oven at 400°F*
• *Food processor (metal blade)* • *Large casserole pan or Dutch oven, high heat*
• *Medium saucepan, medium heat*

Eggs
truffle oil
4 large eggs
2 slices of prosciutto
2 tbsp heavy cream
½ oz Parmesan cheese

Tomato loaf
1 small seeded loaf (14 oz)
2 tbsp sun-dried tomatoes
   packed in oil (from a jar)
1 clove garlic
2 tbsp balsamic vinegar
½ bunch of fresh thyme

Spring greens
4 scallions
olive oil
1 bunch of asparagus (10 oz)
1 tsp mint sauce
1 heaping tsp all-purpose flour
1¼ cups reduced-fat (2%) milk
8 oz frozen petit pois (sweetlet
   peas)
4 large handfuls of baby spinach

Fish
14 oz any undyed smoked white
   fish fillets, scaled and pin-boned
1 lemon

START COOKING

Rub a 5-inch baking dish with 1 teaspoon of truffle oil, then crack in the eggs • Tear the prosciutto slices in half and drape over the egg yolks, then drizzle with the cream • Finely grate over the Parmesan, then put in the oven until the eggs are cooked to your liking

Cut deep crisscrosses into the loaf • Throw the sun-dried tomatoes with 1 teaspoon of their oil, the peeled garlic clove and the balsamic into the processor and blitz to a paste • Pick up the paste with the thyme sprigs, then brush, poke and push everything into the cracks in the bread and pop in the oven

Trim and roughly slice the scallions, then put into the casserole pan with 1 tablespoon of olive oil • Trim the asparagus and add, along with the mint sauce, flour, milk, peas, spinach and a pinch of salt and pepper, then put the lid on and simmer, correcting the seasoning at the end • Pop the fish into the medium saucepan, cover with boiling water and simmer gently (roughly 6 minutes) • When everything's ready, flake the fish over the veg, then serve with lemon wedges, the coddled eggs and crispy tomato loaf

SMOKED SALMON
POTATO & ASPARAGUS SALAD

SERVES 4 | 452 CALORIES

Ingredients out • Kettle boiled • Oven at 325°F
• Small lidded saucepan, high heat • Grill pan, high heat

Potato & asparagus salad

1 lb baby white potatoes
4 rashers of smoked bacon
　or pancetta
1 tsp English mustard
1 heaping tsp grainy mustard
¼ cup fat-free plain yogurt
½ bunch of fresh dill
white wine vinegar
1 red endive

Bread

½ small seeded loaf or wholegrain
　baguette
unsalted butter

Salmon

8 oz quality smoked salmon
1 bunch of asparagus (10 oz)
1 cup sprouted cress or pea shoots
1 lemon

START COOKING

Halving any larger ones, put the potatoes into the small saucepan with a pinch of salt, then cover with boiling water and the lid • Pop the bread into the oven • Put the bacon or pancetta on the grill pan, turning when golden, then remove to a board • Lay the smoked salmon over a nice platter in elegant waves, edge to edge

Lay four asparagus spears flat on a board and, holding each one by the stalk end, peel into delicate ribbons (discarding the woody ends), then scatter over the smoked salmon with the snipped sprouted cress or pea shoots • Trim the remaining asparagus and throw into the pan with the potatoes, then replace the lid

Put the mustards, yogurt, chopped dill and a lug of vinegar into a large shallow serving bowl and season to taste • Drain the potatoes and asparagus and toss into the bowl, then finely slice and sprinkle over the endive and crumble over the crispy bacon or pancetta • Serve with bread, a little butter and lemon wedges

FLASHY FISH STEW
SAFFRON SAUCE & GARLIC BREAD

SERVES 4 | 516 CALORIES

Ingredients out • Kettle boiled • Oven at 425°F • Food processor (metal blade) • Large lidded casserole pan or Dutch oven, medium heat

Garlic bread
1 ciabatta loaf
3–4 cloves garlic
a few sprigs of fresh lemon thyme
1 tbsp extra virgin olive oil

Fish stew
1 bulb fennel
4 anchovy fillets
4 scallions
½–1 fresh red chile
olive oil
2 cloves garlic
½ cup white wine
3 ¼ cups passata
1 small bunch of fresh basil
14 oz mixture of fish fillets,
   scaled and pin-boned. (I like
   striped bass or Pacific cod)
14 oz mussels and clams, scrubbed
   clean and debearded
4 jumbo raw shell-on shrimp

Sauce
1 clove garlic
1 pinch of saffron
3 heaping tbsp fat-free plain
   yogurt
½ lemon

START COOKING

Cut deep crisscrosses into the ciabatta • Squash the unpeeled garlic through a garlic press over the bread, add the thyme sprigs and a pinch of salt and pepper, then drizzle over the extra virgin olive oil • Rub into the cracks of the bread, then put into the oven until golden

Halve the fennel (reserving any leafy tops) and put into the processor with the anchovies, the trimmed scallions and chile, then blitz until finely chopped • Put into the casserole pan with 2 tablespoons of olive oil and turn the heat up to high, stirring regularly • Squash in the unpeeled garlic through a garlic press, then pour the wine into the pan and let it cook away • Pour in the passata and 1⅓ cups of boiling water, tear in most of the basil leaves and season with salt and pepper

Cut the fish up so you've got 4 even-sized chunks of each type, then add all the seafood to the pan (throw away any open mussels and clams that don't close when tapped), cover with the lid and boil • Peel the garlic and bash with a pinch of salt and the saffron in a pestle and mortar, then muddle in the yogurt and a squeeze of lemon juice • When the mussels and clams have opened (throw away any that remain closed), the fish will be cooked through (roughly 4 minutes) • Season to taste, then serve scattered with the remaining basil leaves and fennel tops, the saffron sauce and garlic bread

SEARED ASIAN TUNA
COCONUT RICE & JIGGY JIGGY GREENS

SERVES 4 | 648 CALORIES

Ingredients out • Kettle boiled • Small lidded saucepan, medium-high heat • Large frying pan, medium-high heat • Food processor (fine slicer)

Rice

1 x 14-oz can of light coconut milk

1 coconut milk can or 1 cup
   basmati rice

1 lime

Tuna

1 x 1-lb piece of yellowfin
   tuna steak

2 green tea bags

1 tbsp raw sesame seeds

olive oil

3 tbsp pickled ginger

2 scallions

1 fresh red chile

1 pink grapefruit

reduced-sodium soy sauce

½ bunch of fresh cilantro

Greens

2 bok choy

1 bunch of asparagus (10 oz)

1 bunch of broccolini (7 oz)

2 tsp Asian sesame oil, plus extra
   to serve

3 cloves garlic

1 tbsp Teriyaki sauce

START COOKING

Pour the coconut milk, 1 can's worth of rice and 1 can of boiling water (use a tea towel to hold the can) into the small saucepan • Season with salt and pepper, stir well, cover and cook for roughly 10 minutes, stirring occasionally, then turn the heat off • Halve the tuna lengthways, then empty the contents of the tea bags onto a board with the sesame seeds and a pinch of salt and pepper • Roll and press the tuna in the flavors to coat, then put into the frying pan with 1 tablespoon of olive oil • Sear for about 40 seconds on each side, then remove to a plate, leaving the pan on the heat

Halve the bok choy, then finely slice in the processor with the trimmed asparagus and broccolini • Put the sesame oil into the frying pan and turn the heat up to high • Squash in the unpeeled garlic through a garlic press, then tip in the sliced greens • Toss and move around for 2 minutes, then season to taste with Teriyaki sauce and remove from the heat

Pour the pickled ginger and its juices onto a nice serving platter • Finely slice the trimmed scallions and chile and sprinkle over the top • Squeeze over the grapefruit juice and season to taste • Slice the tuna ½-inch thick and place on the dressing, drizzle with a little soy sauce, then sprinkle with cilantro leaves and a few dribbles of sesame oil • Serve with the rice, lime wedges and greens

WHITE FISH TAGINE
CARROT, CILANTRO & CLEMENTINE SALAD

SERVES 4 | 565 CALORIES

Ingredients out • Kettle boiled • High-sided roasting pan, medium heat • Small frying pan, low heat • Food processor (grater)

Couscous
½ lemon
½ bunch of fresh mint
1 mug (10 oz) of couscous

Tagine
olive oil
2 cloves garlic
1 handful of mixed olives (with pits)
2 tsp harissa
2 anchovy fillets
3 ¼ cups passata
1 small preserved lemon
1 good pinch of saffron
4 x 4-oz sole fillets, skin off
   and pin-boned

Salad
2 tbsp raw sesame seeds
3 medium carrots
3 clementines
1 tbsp extra virgin olive oil
½ lemon
½ bunch of fresh cilantro

To serve
1 tbsp harissa
¼ cup fat-free plain yogurt

START COOKING

Put ½ a lemon, the mint stalks (reserving the top leafy half) and a pinch of salt into a nice serving bowl with 1 mug of couscous and 2 mugs of boiling water, then cover • Drizzle 2 tablespoons of olive oil into the roasting pan and squash in the unpeeled garlic through a garlic press • Stir the olives, harissa, anchovies and passata into the pan, and tear in the preserved lemon

Cover the saffron with a splash of boiling water • Season each fish fillet with salt and pepper, roll up and place in the sauce, then sprinkle the fish with the saffron • Scrunch up and wet a sheet of parchment paper, tuck it over the fish and leave to simmer fast until cooked through (roughly 8 minutes) • Taste and correct the seasoning • Toast the sesame seeds in the frying pan until golden, then remove

Grate the trimmed carrots in the processor and pile onto a serving plate • Peel the clementines, slice into rounds and place on top, then tear over the mint leaves and drizzle with the extra virgin olive oil and lemon juice • Sprinkle over the toasted sesame seeds, season with salt and pepper and toss together • In a small bowl, swirl the harissa through the yogurt • Fluff up the couscous and serve with the fish tagine and carrot salad, sprinkling everything with cilantro leaves

LUCKY SQUID 'N' SHRIMP
SPICY VEGETABLE NOODLE BROTH

Ingredients out • Kettle boiled • Medium lidded casserole pan or Dutch oven, high heat • Food processor (metal blade & thick slicer) • Large grill pan, high heat

Broth
2 chicken bouillon cubes
¼ head of cauliflower
1 red bell pepper
7 oz sugar snap peas
1 bok choy
4 nests of fine egg noodles
2 limes

Paste
1 thumb-sized piece of gingerroot
2 cloves garlic
2 stalks lemongrass
6 kaffir lime leaves
1 fresh red chile
1 bunch of fresh cilantro
1 tbsp honey
1 tbsp fish sauce
1 tbsp reduced-sodium soy sauce, plus extra to serve
1 tbsp Asian sesame oil

Seafood
7 oz squid, gutted and cleaned
7 oz jumbo raw peeled shrimp
5 oz mixed mushrooms
1 tbsp honey

START COOKING

Pour 6 cups of boiling water into the casserole pan and crumble in the bouillon cubes • Peel the ginger, garlic and the outer leaves of the lemongrass, roughly chop them and put into the processor • Add the lime leaves, chile, cilantro stalks, honey, fish and soy sauces and the sesame oil, then whiz until combined

Put 1 heaping tablespoon of that paste in a bowl, then add the rest to the hot broth • Cut open the squid tubes and using a regular eating knife, lightly score the inside in a ¼-inch crisscross, put into the bowl with the squid legs, shrimp and mushrooms, then toss to coat in the paste and put aside • Swap to the thick slicer in the processor and slice the cauliflower, seeded pepper, sugar snaps and bok choy

Stir the noodles and sliced veg into the broth, put the lid on and bring back to a boil for 2 minutes – don't overcook it • Place the squid and mushrooms on the screaming-hot grill pan, sprinkle over the shrimp and cook until lightly charred on both sides, then drizzle with the honey • Season the broth thoughtfully to taste with soy sauce and lime juice, then scatter with the cilantro leaves • Slice up the squid and serve

KOH SAMUI SALAD
CHILI TOFU & THAI NOODLES

SERVES 4 | 680 CALORIES

Ingredients out • Kettle boiled • Medium frying pan, low heat • Food processor (metal blade & fine slicer)

Salad

10 oz medium rice noodles

1 clove garlic

1 thumb-sized piece of gingerroot

6 ripe cherry or grape tomatoes

1 fresh red chile

½ bunch of fresh basil

1 heaping tsp golden brown sugar

3 tbsp fish sauce

2 tbsp Asian sesame oil

3 limes

1 bunch of radishes

2 carrots

½ English cucumber

1 bulb fennel

½ head of white cabbage

3 ½ oz cooked peeled shrimp

Garnishes

3 ½ oz unsalted blanched peanuts

2 tbsp raw sesame seeds

1 tsp Asian sesame oil

3 dried kaffir lime leaves

1 bunch of fresh mint

1 package (11 oz) of silken tofu

1 tbsp sweet red chili sauce

1 lime

START COOKING

Put the noodles in a bowl and cover with boiling water, mixing up regularly to separate • In the frying pan, toast the peanuts and sesame seeds with the sesame oil and crumbled lime leaves until golden, tossing often • Put the peeled garlic and ginger, tomatoes, chile and top leafy half of the basil into the processor with the sugar, fish sauce, sesame oil and juice of 3 limes, then blitz until fine

With the dressing still in the processor, swap to the fine slicer and slice the radishes, trimmed carrots, cucumber, quartered fennel and wedged-up cabbage • Tip it all into a big bowl, scrunch and dress the salad quite roughly with clean hands, then have a taste and tweak the flavors if needed

Drain the noodles, add to the salad bowl with the shrimp, and toss together • Rip off the top leafy half of the mint, roughly chop it and scatter over the top • Cut the tofu into ¾-inch chunks and pile in the middle of the salad drizzled with chili sauce • Scatter over the toasted nuts and serve with lime wedges

BUTTERFLIED SARDINES TUSCAN BREAD SALAD

Ingredients out • Oven broiler on high • Food processor (metal blade)
• Grill pan, high heat

Sardines

1 pinch of saffron
4 scallions
½ fresh red chile
½ bunch of fresh Italian parsley
½ tsp fennel seeds
2 lemons
olive oil
8 fresh sardines, scaled
   and butterflied
4 rashers of smoked bacon
   or pancetta

Salad

½ ciabatta loaf
1 clove garlic
4 anchovy fillets
extra virgin olive oil
3 tbsp balsamic vinegar
1½ lbs ripe heirloom mixed
   tomatoes
½ bunch of scallions
½ bunch of fresh basil
1 tbsp capers (drained)
7 oz roasted red peppers
   (from a jar)
1 oz feta cheese

START COOKING

Put the saffron, trimmed scallions, chile, parsley, fennel seeds, juice of 1 lemon, 1 tablespoon of olive oil, and a pinch of salt and pepper into the processor, then pulse to a coarse paste • Rub the paste over a baking sheet just big enough to lay out the sardines flat on top, skin-side up • Lay the bacon or pancetta in waves between the fish, then grill until golden and crispy (roughly 8 minutes)

Cut four ¾-inch-thick slices of ciabatta and place on the grill pan until toasted on both sides • Peel the garlic and put into the processor with the anchovies, 1 tablespoon of extra virgin olive oil, the balsamic, and half the tomatoes, trimmed scallions and basil • Whiz to a smooth dressing and season nicely to taste, then tip into a large serving bowl

Add the capers to the bowl, then randomly cut up and add the peppers • Tear the ciabatta into thumb-sized pieces, add to the bowl and toss together • Halve or quarter the remaining tomatoes, trim and finely slice the remaining scallions and add, then pick over the rest of the basil leaves • Crumble over the feta, and drizzle with 1 teaspoon of extra virgin olive oil to finish • Serve with the sardines and lemon wedges

CHORIZO & SQUID
GREEK-STYLE COUSCOUS SALAD

SERVES 4 | 634 CALORIES

Ingredients out • Kettle boiled • Food processor (metal blade)
• Large frying pan, high heat

Couscous

4 scallions
2 large handfuls of baby spinach
1 bunch of fresh mint
1 mug (10 oz) of couscous
1 lemon

Chorizo & squid

14 oz baby squid, gutted
  and cleaned
3 oz cured chorizo sausage
olive oil
2 mixed-color bell peppers
1 tbsp honey
sherry vinegar
2 cloves garlic
8–10 black olives (with pits)

Garnishes

1 ¾ oz feta cheese
1 heaping tsp harissa
¼ cup fat-free plain yogurt

START COOKING

Blitz the trimmed scallions in the processor with the spinach, most of the top leafy half of the mint and a pinch of salt and pepper until fine • Remove the blade, stir in 1 mug of couscous and 2 mugs of boiling water, put the lid on and leave to sit in the processor • Cut open the squid tubes and, using a regular eating knife, lightly score the inside in ¼-inch crisscrosses, then slice with a sharp knife about ½-inch thick, and roughly slice the tentacles

Slice the chorizo and put it into the pan with 2 tablespoons of oil • Seed, slice and add the peppers, then about 4 minutes later stir in all the squid, the honey and a splash of vinegar • Squash over the unpeeled garlic through a garlic press, pit and add the olives and stir for a few more minutes

Fluff up the couscous and mix with the juice of ½ a lemon, then tip onto a big board or platter • Spoon the squid, peppers and chorizo over the couscous • Crumble the feta over the top and pick over the remaining mint leaves • In a small bowl, ripple the harissa through the yogurt and serve everything together, with lemon wedges on the side

BAKED WHOLE TROUT
BABY POTATOES, PEAS & MUSTARD SAUCE

SERVES 4 | 504 CALORIES

Ingredients out • Kettle boiled • Oven at full whack (475°F)
• Food processor (thick slicer) • Lidded casserole pan or Dutch oven, high heat

Trout

4 x 8-oz trout fillets, scaled
   and gutted
olive oil
1 lemon
1 bunch of fresh thyme
1 oz sliced almonds
4 rashers of smoked bacon
   or pancetta

Veg

1¼ lbs baby white potatoes
2 chicken bouillon cubes
2 little gem lettuces or hearts
   of romaine
1 bunch of fresh mint
10 oz frozen peas
7 oz frozen fava beans

Sauce

2 tsp grated horseradish (from a jar)
1 tsp English mustard
½ lemon
¼ cup fat-free plain yogurt

START COOKING

On a baking sheet, season the trout with salt, pepper and 1 tablespoon of oil
• Cut the lemon into quarters, add to the pan and cook on the top shelf
of the oven • Slice the baby potatoes in the processor and put into the
casserole pan with 4 cups of boiling water • Crumble in the bouillon cubes,
cover with the lid and boil

In a bowl, mix the horseradish, mustard, juice from ½ a lemon and a small
pinch of salt together, then ripple it through the yogurt • Slice up the
lettuces and finely chop the top leafy half of the mint

Toss the thyme sprigs in 1 teaspoon of oil, then scatter over the trout
with the sliced almonds • Lay a piece of bacon or pancetta over each
fish and put back into the oven for a few minutes, until golden and
crispy • Stir the lettuce, mint leaves, peas and fava beans into the potato
pan • Season to taste, cook for a couple of minutes, then serve with the
crispy trout and mustard sauce

PASTA

PASTA PESTO
GARLIC & ROSEMARY CHICKEN

SERVES 4 | 581 CALORIES

Ingredients out • Kettle boiled • Large frying pan, high heat
• Large lidded casserole pan or Dutch oven, high heat
• Food processor (metal blade)

Chicken

2 x 7-oz skinless boneless chicken
  breasts
1 tsp fennel seeds
2 sprigs of fresh rosemary
2 tbsp canola oil
4–5 cloves garlic
1–2 fresh red chiles
8 ripe cherry or grape tomatoes

Pasta & pesto

8 oz green beans
1 big bunch of fresh basil
2 oz blanched almonds
2 oz Parmesan cheese,
  plus extra to serve
2 tbsp extra virgin olive oil
1 lemon
1 clove garlic
10 oz fresh lasagne sheets
  (roughly 10 sheets)
4 large handfuls of baby spinach

START COOKING

On a large sheet of parchment paper, toss the chicken with salt, pepper, the fennel seeds and rosemary leaves • Fold over the paper, then bash and flatten the chicken to ¾-inch thick with a rolling pin • Put into the frying pan with the canola oil, the bashed unpeeled garlic cloves and halved chiles, turning after about 3 or 4 minutes, until golden and cooked through • Line the beans up and cut off the stem ends, put into the casserole pan, cover with boiling salted water and cook for 6 minutes with the lid on

Pick a few basil leaves for garnish, then rip off the stalks and put the rest of the bunch into the processor with the almonds, Parmesan, extra virgin olive oil and lemon juice • Squash in the unpeeled garlic through a garlic press • Blitz until smooth, adding a ladle or two of cooking water from the beans to loosen, then season to taste • Slice the lasagne sheets up into random handkerchief shapes and add to the beans to cook for a couple of minutes • Halve or quarter the tomatoes, add to the chicken and give the pan a shake

Stir the spinach into the pasta pan, then drain, reserving a cupful of the starchy cooking water • Return the pasta, beans and spinach to the pan, pour in the pesto from the processor and stir together, loosening with splashes of cooking water until silky • Slice the chicken breasts in half and serve with the tomatoes and chile spooned over the top • Finely grate a little extra Parmesan over the pasta, then sprinkle everything with basil leaves

CRAB BOLOGNESE
CRUNCHY FENNEL SALAD

SERVES 4 | 673 CALORIES

Ingredients out • Kettle boiled • Food processor (metal blade & fine slicer)
• Lidded casserole pan or Dutch oven, medium heat
• Large lidded saucepan, high heat

Pasta & sauce

½–1 fresh red chile
1 carrot
2 scallions
2 cloves garlic
1 heaping tsp fennel seeds
2 anchovy fillets
½ bunch of fresh basil
2 bulbs fennel
olive oil
11 oz dried spaghetti
1 lemon
10 oz fresh crabmeat
  (brown and white meat)
white wine
3 ¼ cups passata

Salad

2 little gem lettuces or hearts
  of romaine
½ bunch of fresh mint
1 lemon
Parmesan cheese
1 tbsp extra virgin olive oil

START COOKING

Halve the chile, carrot and trimmed scallions and put them in the processor with the peeled garlic, fennel seeds, anchovies and basil stalks • Chop off and add the top stalky part of the fennel, reserving the bulbs (and any leafy tops), then blitz everything until finely chopped • Tip into the casserole pan with 1 tablespoon of olive oil, stirring often • Put the spaghetti into the large saucepan, cover with boiling salted water and cook following the package instructions

Finely grate the lemon zest over the veg • Add the brown crabmeat, a splash of white wine and the passata, then stir, cover and leave to simmer • Swap to the fine slicer in the processor • Halve the fennel bulbs and trim the lettuces, then slice them in the processor and tip into a salad bowl • Rip off and slice the top leafy half of the mint, and add to the bowl with a pinch of salt and pepper, the juice of 1 lemon and a few shavings of Parmesan

Roughly chop the top leafy half of the basil and sprinkle most of it into the sauce with the white crabmeat, then squeeze in the juice of the zested lemon • Loosen the sauce with a little starchy cooking water from the spaghetti, then drain the spaghetti and tip into a large bowl • Spoon the sauce on top and serve right away, scattered with the reserved basil leaves, mixing at the table, with the crunchy fennel salad on the other side, finishing both with a drizzle of extra virgin olive oil

SAUSAGE FUSILLI
CREAMY GARDEN SALAD

SERVES 4 | 622 CALORIES

Ingredients out • *Kettle boiled* • *Grill pan, high heat* • *Food processor (metal blade)* • *Large frying pan, high heat* • *Large lidded saucepan, high heat*

Pasta

4 good-quality pork sausages
   (preferably higher welfare)
olive oil
1 large red onion
1 heaping tsp fennel seeds
4 roasted red peppers (from a jar)
4 sprigs of fresh rosemary
4 cloves garlic
11 oz dried fusilli
3 tbsp thick balsamic vinegar,
   plus extra to serve
1½ cups passata

Salad

1 head of bibb lettuce
2 large handfuls of baby spinach
   or arugula
1 cup sprouted cress
2 tsp English mustard
3 tbsp fat-free plain yogurt
1 lemon
1 bunch of fresh chives

START COOKING

Score the sausages lengthways about three-quarters of the way through, open them out like a book, then rub with 1 teaspoon of oil and place on the grill pan, cut-side down, turning regularly, until crispy and cooked through • Peel and halve the red onion, then pulse in the processor with the fennel seeds, peppers, half of the rosemary leaves and a pinch of salt and pepper • Put into the large frying pan with 1 tablespoon of oil, squash in the unpeeled garlic through a garlic press and stir frequently

Put the pasta into the saucepan, cover with boiling salted water and cook following the package instructions • Add the balsamic and passata to the veg pan • Trim the lettuce and cut into wedges, then arrange with the spinach or arugula around a nice board or platter and snip over the sprouted cress • Toss the remaining rosemary leaves with the sausages until crispy, then remove from the heat

Make a dressing by mixing the mustard, yogurt and lemon juice with a pinch of salt and pepper • Finely chop the chives, stir half through the dressing, then drizzle over the salad • Drain the pasta, reserving a cupful of the starchy cooking water, then toss well with the sauce, loosening with a splash of cooking water, if needed • Season to taste and tip onto a platter, scatter over the remaining chives, chop and scatter over the sausages and finish with a drizzle of balsamic from a height

CHORIZO CARBONARA
CATALAN MARKET SALAD

SERVES 4 | 603 CALORIES

Ingredients out • *Kettle boiled* • *Large frying pan, medium heat*
• *Large lidded saucepan, high heat*

Salad

1 oz pine nuts
1 red endive
1 green endive
2 clementines
2 large handfuls of baby spinach
4 sprigs of fresh mint
1½ oz Manchego cheese
2 tbsp sherry vinegar
2 tbsp extra virgin olive oil
1 tsp honey

Pasta

11 oz dried penne
2 ½ oz cured chorizo
½–1 fresh red chile
2 sprigs of fresh rosemary
olive oil
4 cloves garlic
1 large egg
½ lemon
2 heaping tbsp fat-free
   plain yogurt

START COOKING

Toast the pine nuts in the frying pan for a few minutes, tossing often • Put the pasta into the saucepan, cover with boiling salted water and cook following the package instructions • Finely slice the stalk ends of the endive and break apart the upper leaves into a serving bowl • Peel and finely slice the clementines, add to the bowl with the baby spinach, then pick over the mint leaves • Shave over a tiny bit of Manchego and scatter with the hot nuts, returning the frying pan to a medium heat

In a cup, make your dressing with the vinegar, extra virgin olive oil and honey, then season to taste and put aside • Finely slice the chorizo, chile and rosemary leaves and put into the frying pan with 1 teaspoon of olive oil and a pinch of pepper, then squash in the unpeeled garlic through a garlic press and move everything around until lightly golden

Beat the egg, lemon juice, yogurt and remaining finely grated Manchego together in a bowl • Drain the pasta, reserving a cupful of the starchy cooking water • Toss the pasta into the chorizo pan, remove from the heat and mix well with the creamy sauce, loosening with a splash of cooking water, if needed, then season to taste • Dress and toss the salad, then serve with the pasta

WINTER SQUASH PENNE
MINT & AVOCADO CHOPPED SALAD

SERVES 4 | 635 CALORIES

Pasta

1 vegetable bouillon cube
1 butternut squash (neck end only)
1 onion
1 tsp fennel seeds
1 small dried red chile
½ bunch of fresh sage
1 x 14-oz can of chickpeas
11 oz dried penne
1 oz Parmesan cheese,
  plus extra to serve
½ bunch of fresh Italian parsley

Salad

3 ripe tomatoes
½ English cucumber
4 scallions
2 little gem lettuces or hearts
  of romaine
½ bunch of fresh mint
1 ripe avocado
2 tbsp extra virgin olive oil
2 tbsp balsamic vinegar
¾ oz feta cheese

Ingredients out • Kettle boiled • Food processor (metal blade) • Lidded casserole pan or Dutch oven, medium heat • Large lidded saucepan, high heat • Immersion blender

START COOKING

Make 2 cups of hot broth with the cube, then refill and boil the kettle • Trim the stalk off the squash, roughly chop the neck end (don't peel, and keep the seed end for another day), then blitz in the processor with the peeled onion, fennel seeds, dried chile and sage leaves until combined • Put into the casserole pan, add the broth and the chickpeas and their juice, then put the lid on and stir regularly

Put the pasta into the large saucepan, cover with boiling salted water and cook following the package instructions • On a large board, chop and mix up the tomatoes, cucumber, trimmed scallions, lettuce and the top leafy half of the mint • Squeeze and squidge over the avocado, discarding the skin and pit • Dress and toss with the extra virgin olive oil and balsamic, then season to taste and crumble over the feta

Using an immersion blender, blitz the sauce to your liking, season well to taste and finely grate in the Parmesan • Drain the pasta, toss with the sauce and season to taste • Serve scattered with chopped parsley leaves and an extra grating of Parmesan

SIMPLE SPAGHETTI
TOMATO, BASIL & CREAMY CURD SALAD

SERVES 4 | 553 CALORIES

Ingredients out • *Kettle boiled* • *Large lidded saucepan, high heat*
• *Large roasting pan, low heat*

Pasta

11 oz dried spaghetti
1½ bunches of broccolini (10 oz)
½–1 fresh red chile
8 anchovy fillets
4 cloves garlic
2 sprigs of fresh rosemary
1 lemon
optional: Parmesan cheese

Salad

1 lb ripe heirloom mixed tomatoes
a few sprigs of fresh basil
extra virgin olive oil
1 tbsp balsamic vinegar
1 lemon
½ cup low-fat cottage cheese

START COOKING

Put the pasta into the large saucepan, cover with boiling salted water and cook following the package instructions • Roughly chop the tomatoes and put them into a bowl • Tear in most of the basil leaves, add 1 tablespoon of oil and the balsamic, then toss and season to taste • Grate the zest of 1 lemon into a nice smallish serving bowl, then squeeze in half the juice • Stir in the cottage cheese, then top with your dressed tomatoes and a few small basil leaves

Trim the broccolini and halve the stalks lengthways, then finely slice the chile • Turn the heat under the roasting pan up to medium-high and add ¼ cup of oil, the chile and anchovies • Squash in the unpeeled garlic through a garlic press, strip in the rosemary leaves and add the broccolini, then add a splash of pasta water • Use tongs to shake and move everything around

Drain the pasta, reserving a cupful of the starchy cooking water, then toss the pasta with the broccolini, the juice of a lemon and enough cooking water to make it shiny • Season to taste, and serve with a grating of Parmesan, if you like, and the tomato, basil and creamy curd salad on the side

SAUSAGE GNOCCHI
WARM KALE & BEAN SALAD

SERVES 4 | 526 CALORIES

Ingredients out • Kettle boiled • Large casserole pan or Dutch oven, high heat • Small frying pan, high heat • Large lidded saucepan, high heat • Food processor (thick slicer)

Gnocchi

4 spicy good-quality pork sausages
   (preferably higher welfare)
2 tsp fennel seeds
2 sprigs of fresh rosemary
½ cup Chianti or other light-bodied
   dry red wine
1 bunch of broccolini (7 oz)
3 ¼ cups passata
14 oz gnocchi
2 tbsp fat-free plain yogurt

Greens

2 rashers of smoked bacon
olive oil
⅓ cup blanched hazelnuts
1 tsp maple syrup or honey
7 oz fine green beans
10 oz mixed greens, such as curly
   kale, Swiss chard, cavolo nero
   and spring greens
1½ tbsp extra virgin olive oil
1½ tbsp sherry vinegar

START COOKING

Squeeze the sausage meat out of the casings into the casserole pan with the fennel seeds and rosemary leaves (discard the casings) • Break the meat apart, stirring regularly • Finely slice the bacon, put into the small frying pan with 1 teaspoon of olive oil and the hazelnuts and cook until golden, then add the maple syrup or honey and remove from the heat

Line the beans up and cut off the stem ends, then put them into the large saucepan, cover with boiling salted water and the lid • Cook for 4 minutes, then add the greens, tearing up any larger leaves • Pour the wine into the sausage pan and let it bubble away while you check on the beans and greens • If done, use a slotted spoon to transfer them to a colander to drain, leaving the pan of water on the heat • Tear the broccolini tips into the sausage pan, then slice and add the stalks, along with the passata

Add the gnocchi to the pan of water the greens were cooked in and pop the lid on • Mix the extra virgin olive oil, vinegar and a pinch of salt and pepper in a serving bowl, tip in the drained greens and toss to coat, then scatter over the crispy nuts and bacon • When the gnocchi have been floating for a couple of minutes, drain them and toss with the sauce • Season to taste and serve in the pan, or on a nice platter, drizzled with yogurt

CHICKEN CACCIATORE
SPAGHETTI & SMOKY TOMATO SAUCE

Ingredients out · Kettle boiled · Large frying pan, medium heat
· Large lidded saucepan, medium heat

Chicken & sauce

4 skinless boneless chicken thighs
olive oil
4 oz oyster mushrooms
4 oz cremini mushrooms
4 rashers of smoked bacon or
   pancetta
2–3 sprigs of fresh rosemary
2 anchovy fillets
2 roasted red peppers (from a jar)
1 small handful of black olives
   (with pits)
2 cloves garlic
1 fresh red chile
¼ cup Chianti or other light-bodied
   dry red wine
3 ¼ cups passata
1 bunch of fresh basil

Pasta

11 oz dried wholewheat spaghetti
1 oz Parmesan cheese

START COOKING

Cut the chicken into ½-inch chunks, then put into the large frying pan with 2 tablespoons of oil and a pinch of salt and pepper · Roughly chop the mushrooms, finely slice the bacon or pancetta, then add both to the pan with the rosemary leaves, anchovies and torn-up peppers · Squash and add the olives (discarding the pits), then turn the heat up to medium-high, tossing regularly until golden

Put the pasta into the large saucepan, cover with boiling salted water and cook following the package instructions · Squash the unpeeled garlic through a garlic press into the chicken pan · Finely slice and add the chile, pour in the wine and passata, then season to taste · Tear in and stir through most of the top leafy half of the basil

Finely grate the Parmesan · Drain the pasta, reserving a cupful of the starchy cooking water, then tip onto a platter and spoon over the sauce · Scatter with the remaining basil leaves and the grated Parmesan · Toss together, loosening with a splash of cooking water, if needed

FETTUCCINE
SMOKED TROUT, ASPARAGUS & PEAS

SERVES 4 | 687 CALORIES

Ingredients out • Kettle boiled • Medium saucepan, high heat
• Large lidded saucepan, high heat • Immersion blender

Pasta

1 small bunch of scallions
1 bunch of asparagus (10 oz)
olive oil
10 oz frozen peas
1 big bunch of fresh mint
1 tbsp all-purpose flour
2 cups reduced-fat (2%) milk
11 oz dried fettuccine
8 oz hot-smoked trout
Parmesan cheese, to serve

Salad & dressing

1 red endive
1 green endive
1 little gem lettuce or heart of
    romaine
a few sprigs of fresh tarragon
2 heaping tsp Dijon mustard
1 heaping tsp honey
1 tbsp extra virgin olive oil
1 lemon
1 heaping tbsp fat-free
    plain yogurt

START COOKING

Roughly slice the trimmed scallions and asparagus stalks (leave the tips whole and put aside), and put into the medium saucepan with 2 tablespoons of olive oil and the peas • Roughly chop most of the top leafy half of the mint, and add it to the pan • Stir in the flour, pour in the milk and bring to a boil, then simmer • Put the pasta into the large saucepan, cover with boiling salted water and cook following the package instructions

Cut the endive and lettuce into long thin wedges and put these into a salad bowl • Pick over the tarragon and the remaining mint leaves • Spoon the mustard and honey into a small bowl, add the extra virgin olive oil, the juice of ½ a lemon and the yogurt, mix together and season to taste

Using the immersion blender, purée the asparagus sauce until fairly smooth • Turn the heat down to low, flake in the trout, add the asparagus tips and simmer for a few more minutes, then squeeze in the rest of the lemon juice and season to taste • Drain the pasta, reserving a cupful of starchy cooking water, then toss the pasta with the sauce, loosening with a splash of cooking water, if needed • Serve straight away, with a grating of Parmesan and the salad, dressing it at the table

CHICKEN PASTA
HERBY 6-VEG RAGÙ

SERVES 4 | 620 CALORIES

Ingredients out • Kettle boiled • Food processor (metal blade) • Large casserole pan or Dutch oven, high heat • Large lidded saucepan, medium heat • Medium frying pan, high heat

Ragù
1 large leek
1 celery stalk
1 carrot
1 zucchini
3 roasted red peppers (from a jar)
olive oil
8 sprigs of fresh thyme
3 ¼ cups passata

Pasta
11 oz dried wholewheat fusilli
2 x 5-oz skinless boneless chicken breasts
3 rashers of smoked bacon
½ fresh red chile
4 cloves garlic
2 sprigs of fresh rosemary
2 fresh bay leaves
1 tbsp pine nuts
balsamic vinegar
Parmesan cheese, to serve

START COOKING

Split the leek lengthways, rinse under the cold tap, then finely chop in the processor with the trimmed celery and carrot, the zucchini and peppers • Put the veg into the casserole pan with 1 tablespoon of oil, the thyme leaves and a pinch of salt and pepper and stir regularly • Put the pasta into the large saucepan, cover with boiling salted water and cook according to the package instructions

Dice the chicken into ¾-inch chunks and put into the frying pan with 1 tablespoon of oil and a pinch of salt and pepper, tossing regularly until golden and cooked through • Stir the passata into the vegetables and simmer • Finely slice the bacon and chile and add to the golden chicken, then squash in the unpeeled garlic through a garlic press • Strip in the rosemary leaves, add the bay leaves and pine nuts, and fry for a minute or two, until the bacon is golden, then drizzle with balsamic

Season the sauce, drain the pasta, reserving a cupful of starchy cooking water, then toss the pasta with the sauce, loosening with the cooking water, if needed, and pour onto a platter • Scatter the chicken and bacon on top of the pasta and serve with a grating of Parmesan

BROCCOLI PASTA
CHOPPED GARDEN SALAD

SERVES 4 | 644 CALORIES

Ingredients out • Kettle boiled • Large lidded casserole pan or Dutch oven, high heat • Blender • Small frying pan, low heat

Pasta
11 oz dried orecchiette
1 bunch of fresh basil
1 x 2-oz can of anchovy
   fillets in oil
1 lemon
2 cloves garlic
1 dried red chile
1 oz Parmesan cheese,
   plus extra to serve
1 large head of broccoli
2 oz pine nuts

Salad
2 carrots
1 ripe avocado
3 ripe heirloom mixed tomatoes
2 tbsp extra virgin olive oil
2 tbsp balsamic vinegar
2 ½ oz arugula

START COOKING

Put the pasta into the casserole pan, cover with boiling salted water and cook following the package instructions • Put the basil, anchovies and 1 tablespoon of their oil, the zest and juice of 1 lemon and a splash of boiling water into the blender • Squash in the unpeeled garlic through a garlic press, crumble in the dried chile, finely grate in the Parmesan and whiz until smooth, then pour into a large bowl • Cut the florets off the broccoli, add to the pasta pan and put the lid on

Using a box grater, coarsely grate the broccoli stalk and carrots onto a board • Squeeze and squidge over the avocado, discarding the skin and pit • Roughly chop the tomatoes • Season the salad with salt and pepper, then drizzle with the extra virgin olive oil and balsamic • Add the arugula and toss together

Toast the pine nuts in the frying pan, turning the heat up, and removing when lightly golden • Drain the pasta and broccoli in a colander, reserving a cupful of the starchy cooking water, then tip into the bowl of sauce • Toss together, loosening with a little cooking water, if needed • Pour onto a platter, finely grate over some extra Parmesan, scatter over the toasted pine nuts and serve

SHRIMP LINGUINE
SICILIAN SHAVED FENNEL SALAD

SERVES 4 | 562 CALORIES

Ingredients out • Kettle boiled • Food processor (metal blade & fine slicer)
• Large non-stick frying pan, medium-high heat
• Large lidded saucepan, medium heat

Bread crumbs
2 slices of rustic bread
2 cloves garlic
extra virgin olive oil

Pasta
11 oz dried linguine
1 fresh red chile
4 anchovy fillets
1 good pinch of ground cinnamon
1 pinch of saffron
12 oz large raw peeled shrimp
2 cloves garlic
2 cups passata
1 lemon
1 oz Parmesan cheese
a couple sprigs of fresh basil

Salad
1 bulb fennel
½ celery heart
1 bunch of fresh mint
1 lemon

START COOKING

Put the bread and peeled garlic into the processor with 1 tablespoon of oil and blitz into bread crumbs • Toast these in the large frying pan until golden, tossing regularly • Put the pasta into the large saucepan, cover with boiling salted water and cook following the package instructions • Swap to the fine slicer in your processor and slice the halved fennel, trimmed celery, the top leafy half of the mint and the whole lemon • Tip into a serving bowl and toss with 1 tablespoon of oil and a pinch of salt and pepper

Tip the bread crumbs into a small bowl and put the pan back on a low heat • Finely chop the chile and put into the frying pan with the anchovies and a little of their oil, the cinnamon, saffron and shrimp, then turn up the heat • Squash in the unpeeled garlic through a garlic press, add the passata and bring to a boil

Squeeze the lemon juice into the frying pan, then use tongs to transfer the spaghetti straight into the sauce • Finely grate in the Parmesan, toss to coat, then season to taste • Transfer the pasta to a platter, loosening with a splash of cooking water, if needed, pick over the basil leaves and serve with the bread crumbs and salad on the side

MUSHROOM FARFALLE
BLUE CHEESE, HAZELNUT & APPLE SALAD

SERVES 4 | 586 CALORIES

Pasta

1 oz dried porcini mushrooms
olive oil
2–4 cloves garlic
½ small dried chile
8 oz cremini mushrooms
6 sprigs of fresh thyme
11 oz dried farfalle
1 tsp truffle oil
1 lemon
½ bunch of fresh Italian parsley
⅔ cup low-fat cottage cheese

Salad

½ cup blanched hazelnuts
4 large handfuls of baby spinach
1 eating apple
1½ oz blue cheese
1 tsp extra virgin olive oil

Ingredients out • *Kettle boiled* • *Large frying pan, medium-high heat*
• *Large lidded saucepan, high heat* • *Small frying pan, medium heat*
• *Food processor (metal blade)*

START COOKING

Put the porcini into a small bowl and just cover with boiling water • Put 2 tablespoons of olive oil into the large frying pan, squash in the unpeeled garlic through a garlic press, crumble in the dried chile and tear in the cremini mushrooms • Strip in the thyme leaves, then add the soaked porcini and toss and fry for a few minutes • Put the pasta into the large saucepan, cover with boiling salted water and cook following the package instructions

Toast the hazelnuts in the small frying pan until golden, tossing regularly • Put the spinach into a salad bowl, coarsely grate over or matchstick and add the apple, then crumble over the blue cheese • Crush the toasted nuts in a pestle and mortar, then scatter over the salad • Tip the mushrooms into the processor and whiz until fairly smooth, then return to the pan and add 3 small ladles of pasta cooking water and the truffle oil, season to taste and simmer gently

Drain the pasta, reserving a cupful of the starchy cooking water, then toss the pasta with the sauce, loosening with a splash of cooking water, if needed • Finely grate over the lemon zest, finely chop and add most of the top leafy half of the parsley along with the cottage cheese, then toss together and serve straight away • Drizzle the salad with extra virgin olive oil, squeeze over the juice of the zested lemon and serve on the side

SALSA VERDE TUNA
SICILIAN TOMATO & PASTA SALAD

SERVES 4 | 651 CALORIES

Ingredients out • Kettle boiled • Large lidded saucepan, high heat • Food processor (metal blade) • Large frying pan, medium heat

Pasta & tuna

11 oz dried pasta shells

8 black olives (with pits)

14 oz ripe heirloom mixed
    tomatoes

4 roasted red peppers (from a jar)

2 ½ oz arugula

4 x 4-oz yellowfin tuna steaks

1 tsp dried oregano

1 tsp fennel seeds

olive oil

1 fresh red chile

1 oz Parmesan cheese

1 lemon

Salsa verde

1 big bunch of fresh mint

1 big bunch of fresh Italian parsley

1 lemon

2 anchovy fillets

2 tsp capers (drained)

1 clove garlic

¼ cup extra virgin olive oil

1 heaping tsp Dijon mustard

1 tbsp white wine vinegar

START COOKING

Put the pasta into the large saucepan, cover with boiling salted water and cook following the package instructions • Rip the top leafy half of the mint and parsley into the processor, squeeze in the lemon juice, add all the other salsa verde ingredients (peel the garlic) and blitz until fine, then season to taste, loosen with 2 tablespoons of water and set aside

Squash the olives (discarding the pits), randomly cut up the tomatoes and peppers, and put them all into a large bowl, then roughly chop and pile the arugula on top • Rub the tuna with salt, pepper, the oregano and fennel seeds, then drizzle with 1 tablespoon of olive oil, put into the frying pan and cook for 1½ minutes on each side, ideally so the tuna's blushing in the middle

Drain the pasta, reserving a cupful of the starchy cooking water, then add to the tomato bowl, toss with half of the salsa verde, loosening with a splash of cooking water, if needed, then pour onto a nice platter • Put the tuna on top, spoon over the remaining salsa verde, scatter with the finely sliced chile, then shave over a little Parmesan with a vegetable peeler and serve with lemon wedges

PESTO SPAGHETTI
LEMON-STEAMED FISH

SERVES 4 | 649 CALORIES

Ingredients out • Kettle boiled • Wok or large frying pan, medium heat • Large lidded saucepan, medium heat • Food processor (metal blade) • Two 10-inch bamboo steamers

Fish
½ lb large sea scallops
14 oz white fish fillets,
   scaled and pin-boned
olive oil
1 lemon
½ dried red chile

Pasta
11 oz dried spaghetti
7 oz green beans
1 bunch of broccolini (7 oz)

Pesto
2 ½ oz blanched almonds
1 big bunch of fresh basil
1 clove garlic
2 tbsp extra virgin olive oil
2 oz Parmesan cheese
1 lemon

START COOKING

Score the scallops on one side in deep crisscrosses • Pour 1 inch of boiling water into the wok or large frying pan • Pour the rest of the water into the other pan, add the spaghetti and a pinch of salt and cook following the package instructions • Put the almonds into the processor, rip in most of the basil leaves and squash in the unpeeled garlic through a garlic press • Add the extra virgin olive oil, Parmesan and the juice from ½ a lemon, blitz until smooth, then season to taste and check the balance of flavors – it should be clean and refreshing

Line the beans up and cut off the stem ends, then add to the pasta pan • Put one of the steamers into the wok and add the trimmed broccolini, then put the second steamer on top • Rub the fish and scallops with a pinch of salt and pepper and lay in the second steamer • Drizzle with 1 tablespoon of olive oil, finely grate over the zest of a lemon and squeeze over half the juice, then crumble over the chile and put the steamer lid on until cooked through

Drain the pasta and beans, reserving a cupful of the starchy cooking water, then return them to the pan • Spoon in the pesto from the processor and toss together, loosening with splashes of the cooking water until silky • Squeeze in lemon juice to taste, then pour into a serving bowl with the broccolini • Sprinkle over the remaining basil leaves and serve alongside the steamer basket of fish

SOUPS & SARNIES

MEXICAN TOMATO SOUP
CHILI NACHOS, VEGGIE & FETA SPRINKLES

Ingredients out • Kettle boiled • Oven broiler on high
• Large lidded saucepan, high heat • Immersion blender

Soup

1 small bunch of scallions
olive oil
1 bunch of fresh cilantro
4 cloves garlic
½ cup basmati rice
1 lb roasted red peppers (from a jar)
2 x 14-oz cans of diced tomatoes
1 cup fat-free plain yogurt
2 tsp pickled jalapeño chiles
½ bunch of fresh mint
2 limes

Sprinkles

1 handful of cherry or grape
    tomatoes
1 ripe avocado
1 oz feta cheese

Nachos

2–3 fresh red and green chiles
3 large handfuls of reduced-sodium
    tortilla chips
2 oz Cheddar cheese

START COOKING

Trim and finely slice the scallions (reserving some for garnish) and put into the saucepan with 2 tablespoons of oil • Tear in the cilantro stalks (reserving the leaves) • Squash in the unpeeled garlic through a garlic press and add the rice, drained jarred peppers, and the canned tomatoes • Pour in 3 ½ cups of boiling water, add a pinch of salt and cover with the lid

Quarter the tomatoes, halve the avocado (discarding the pit) and place on a serving board with the reserved scallions and cilantro leaves, and the feta • Finely slice the chiles and add half to the board • Empty the tortilla chips onto a baking sheet, grate over the Cheddar and scatter over the remaining chiles, then pop under the broiler on the top shelf until the cheese is melted, removing when golden

In a bowl, use the immersion blender to blitz the yogurt and jalapeño chiles with a splash of their pickling vinegar and the top leafy half of the mint until nice and smooth • Next use the immersion blender to blitz the soup until smooth, add the juice of ½ a lime, season well to taste, then either enjoy it thick or add some water to thin it down • Drizzle over the spiked yogurt, and serve with the nachos, sprinkles and lime wedges

MINESTRONE
POACHED CHICKEN & SALSA VERDE

SERVES 4 | 608 CALORIES

Ingredients out • Kettle boiled • Large lidded casserole pan or Dutch oven, medium heat • Food processor (thick slicer & metal blade)

Chicken & soup

6 rashers of smoked bacon
   or pancetta
olive oil
2 sprigs of fresh rosemary
2 small carrots
2 celery stalks
1 red onion
2 chicken bouillon cubes
½ head of broccoli
½ head of cauliflower
½ cup basmati rice
¾ cup dried macaroni (elbows)
2 x 5-oz skinless boneless chicken
   breasts
1 handful of frozen fava beans
1 handful of frozen peas
4 large handfuls of baby spinach
Parmesan cheese, to serve

Salsa verde

1 bunch of fresh tarragon
   or Italian parsley
1 bunch of fresh mint
2 anchovy fillets
1 tbsp cornichons
1 tbsp capers (drained)
1 heaping tsp Dijon mustard
1 clove garlic
3 tbsp extra virgin olive oil
1 tbsp cider vinegar

START COOKING

Finely slice the bacon or pancetta and put it into the casserole pan with 2 tablespoons of olive oil, strip in the rosemary leaves and cook until crispy, then remove it all to a bowl, leaving the oil behind • Take the pan off the heat • Slice the trimmed carrots and celery and peeled onion in the processor then tip into the pan • Put back on a high heat, add salt, pepper and crumble in the bouillon cubes • Slice the broccoli stalks (reserving the florets) and all of the cauliflower in the processor and tip into the pan along with the rice and macaroni, then cover with 6 cups of boiling water and the lid

On a plastic board, bash the fatter end of the chicken breasts with a rolling pin so they're an even thickness, then add to the pan, making sure they're fully submerged, and cover with the lid • Swap to the metal blade in the processor • Put the tarragon or parsley, the top leafy half of the mint, the anchovies, cornichons, capers and mustard in the processor • Squash in the unpeeled garlic through a garlic press and blitz until fine • Scrape into a bowl, add 1 tablespoon of the soup broth, the extra virgin olive oil and vinegar and mix together, loosening with an extra splash of broth, if needed

After about 8 minutes, scoop out the cooked chicken, then add the broccoli florets, fava beans, peas and spinach to the soup, replacing the lid • Spoon the salsa verde onto a platter, slice the chicken breasts, then serve them on top of the salsa, sprinkled with the crispy bacon or pancetta and rosemary • Add more boiling water to the soup if you prefer it brothy, then serve with a few shavings of Parmesan, mixing everything together at the table

MUSHROOM SOUP
STILTON, APPLE & WALNUT CROÛTES

SERVES 4 | 405 CALORIES

Ingredients out • Kettle boiled • Oven broiler on high • Large lidded saucepan, medium heat • Grill pan, high heat • Immersion blender

Soup

2 onions
olive oil
1 chicken or vegetable bouillon
  cube
½ bunch of fresh thyme
2 cloves garlic
4 large portobello mushrooms
½ cup basmati rice
1 tbsp heavy cream
1 tsp truffle oil

Croûtes

8 cremini mushrooms
1 ciabatta loaf
1 clove garlic
1 eating apple
½ bunch of fresh curly parsley
1 lemon
2 oz Stilton cheese
1 small handful of raw walnut
  halves

START COOKING

Peel, halve and finely slice the onions and put them into the large saucepan with 2 tablespoons of olive oil • Crumble in the bouillon cube, add a pinch of salt and pepper, strip in the thyme leaves and squash in 2 unpeeled cloves of garlic through a garlic press • Remove stems from cremini mushrooms and place the tops on the grill pan, turning when charred • Tear the cremini stalks and portobellos into the onion pan, add the rice and cook for a couple of minutes • Pour in 4 cups of boiling water and boil with the lid on

Cut 4 slices of ciabatta at an angle and add to the grill pan • When charred on both sides, rub with a halved garlic clove • Coarsely grate or slice the apple into matchsticks and toss with the roughly chopped parsley and a little lemon juice • Place the cremini mushrooms on the toasts, crumble over the stilton and walnuts, then pop under the broiler until the cheese is melted

Use the immersion blender to purée the soup to a consistency you like, then season to taste, if needed, and swirl in the cream and truffle oil • Top the toasts with pinches of apple and parsley and serve on the side

SQUASH SOUP
SAGEY CHESTNUT DUMPLINGS

SERVES 4 | 484 CALORIES

Ingredients out • Kettle boiled • Food processor (metal blade)
• Large lidded casserole pan or Dutch oven, medium heat • Large lidded
saucepan, high heat • Immersion blender

Soup

1 bunch of scallions
a few sprigs of fresh rosemary
1 fresh red chile
1 chicken bouillon cube
olive oil
1 medium butternut squash
    (neck end only)
3 carrots
1 x 14-oz can of chickpeas

Dumplings

1 small package (3 ½ oz) of
    ready-to-eat chestnuts
heaping ⅔ cup self-rising flour,
    plus extra for dusting
1 chicken bouillon cube
8 rashers of smoked bacon or
    pancetta
10 fresh sage leaves
1 whole nutmeg, for grating
optional: 1 oz Cheddar cheese

START COOKING

Trim the scallions and blitz in the processor with the rosemary leaves, chile and bouillon cube until fine, then put into the casserole pan with 1 tablespoon of oil • Cut the neck off the squash, trimming away the stalky end, then carefully quarter (don't peel, and keep the seed end for another day) • Blitz the squash in the processor with the trimmed carrots until finely chopped • Add to the casserole pan with the chickpeas, their water, and 4 cups of boiling water • Cover with the lid and cook on high • Refill and boil the kettle

Blitz the chestnuts, flour, bouillon cube and a pinch of pepper in the processor • Start adding ⅓ cup of cold water, a splash at a time, until it just comes together as a ball of firm dough • Split the dough in half and roll each piece into a sausage shape on a flour-dusted surface, then cut into ¾-inch chunks • Fill the large saucepan with boiling water, add the dumplings, cover with the lid and simmer on a medium heat for 6 minutes, or until fluffy

Blitz the soup with the immersion blender until lovely and smooth, then season to taste and simmer until ready to serve • Put the bacon or pancetta into a deep roasting pan on a high heat with 1 tablespoon of oil • When it starts to crisp up, add the sage leaves • Scoop out the fluffy dumplings with a slotted spoon, toss in the pan of crispy bacon or pancetta and sage, then finely grate over half the nutmeg and serve with a grating of Cheddar, if you like

MEXICAN BLT
CHILES, GUACAMOLE & SALAD

SERVES 4 | 638 CALORIES

Ingredients out • Oven at 250°F • Medium frying pan, medium-high heat • Food processor (metal blade)

BLT
4 rashers of smoked bacon or pancetta
2 x 6-oz skinless boneless chicken breasts
1 pinch of dried oregano
1 pinch of cumin seeds
1 baguette

Salad
1 little gem lettuce or heart of romaine
1 bunch of radishes
2 cups sprouted cress
1½ oz feta cheese
2 tbsp red wine vinegar
2 tbsp extra virgin olive oil
8 pickled green chiles

Guacamole
½ bunch of fresh cilantro
1 fresh red chile
4 scallions
2 ripe avocados
5 ripe cherry or grape tomatoes
2 limes

START COOKING

Put the bacon or pancetta into the frying pan, removing when golden • On a large sheet of parchment paper, toss the chicken with salt, pepper, the oregano and cumin • Fold over the paper and bash and flatten the chicken to about ¾-inch thick with a rolling pin • Add the chicken to the pan, turning after 3 to 4 minutes, until golden and cooked through • Pop the baguette into the oven • Cut the lettuce into wedges, halve the radishes and pile on a board, then snip over the cress and crumble over the feta

Mix the vinegar, extra virgin olive oil and a pinch of salt and pepper in a small bowl and pop on the board with a pile of pickled chiles • In the processor, pulse most of the cilantro, the chile and trimmed scallions until fairly fine • Squash out and add the avocado flesh (discarding the skin and pits) along with the tomatoes, then squeeze in the juice from 1½ limes, pulse again, and season to taste

Return the crispy bacon or pancetta to the chicken pan to warm through • Get the bread out of the oven and cut it in half lengthways • Spoon the guacamole over the bread, tear over one of the lettuce wedges, slice up and add the chicken and bacon or pancetta and drizzle over any pan juices, then scatter with the remaining cilantro leaves • Serve with lime wedges, pickled chiles and the salad, dressing it at the table

THE BEST FISH BAPS
MUSHY PEAS & TARTARE SAUCE

Ingredients out • Kettle boiled • Oven at 250°F • Small lidded saucepan, high heat • Large frying pan, high heat • Food processor (metal blade)

Baps

4 nice soft wholewheat buns
4 large (halved) or 8 small flat-fish
   fillets (roughly 1 lb in total), such
   as sole or pickerel, skin off and
   pin-boned
1 pinch of cayenne pepper
½ mug (5 oz) of all-purpose flour
olive oil
1 oz Parmesan cheese
1 cup sprouted cress
1 lemon

Peas

1 medium potato
1 lb frozen peas
½ bunch of fresh mint

Sauce

6 cornichons
1 tbsp capers (drained)
1 little gem lettuce or heart of
   romaine
1 cup fat-free plain yogurt
¼ bunch of fresh Italian parsley
1 lemon

START COOKING

Put the buns into the oven • Slice the potato ¼-inch thick, put it into the small saucepan, cover with boiling water and the lid and bring to a boil • On a sheet of parchment paper, season the fish with salt, pepper and the cayenne, then sprinkle over the flour to coat

Pour 2 tablespoons of oil into the frying pan and add the fish • Cook until golden, finely grating the Parmesan over the top when you flip it over • Tip the frozen peas into the pan with the potato, then rip in the leafy top half of the mint and replace the lid

Put the cornichons, capers, lettuce and yogurt into the processor • Tear in the top leafy half of the parsley, squeeze in the lemon juice, then whiz up, season to taste and pour into a bowl • Drain the peas and potatoes, purée in the processor and season to taste • When the fish is perfect, get the buns out of the oven and serve with the peas, tartare sauce, pinches of sprouted cress and lemon wedges

GRILLED MUSHROOM SUB
SMOKY BACON, MELTED CHEESE & PEARS

Ingredients out • Oven broiler on high • Grill pan, high heat

Sub

1 ciabatta loaf
4 large portobello mushrooms
2 oz Emmental cheese
½ bunch of fresh thyme
½ clove garlic
2 ripe pears
8 rashers of smoked bacon or
  pancetta
1 tsp honey
2 large ripe tomatoes
½ cup low-fat cottage cheese
½ lemon

Salad

1 head of bibb lettuce
1 red endive
4 cups watercress
1 bunch of radishes
1 handful of raw walnut halves
5 cornichons
1 tbsp white wine vinegar
2 tbsp extra virgin olive oil
1 tsp Dijon mustard

START COOKING

Place the ciabatta beneath the broiler • Cut off and discard the mushroom stalks, then lay the tops on the grill pan • Quarter the lettuce, finely slice the base of the endive and break the upper leaves apart, then put both in a large bowl with the watercress and halved radishes • Crumble over the walnuts, then chop and add the cornichons

In a separate bowl, mix the vinegar with the oil, mustard, salt and pepper • Transfer the mushrooms to a roasting pan, then slice and lay over the Emmental • Pick over the thyme leaves, squash over the unpeeled garlic through a garlic press and pop under the broiler until the cheese is melted

Quarter the pears and put on the grill pan, turning when golden and adding the bacon or pancetta to the pan to crisp up at the same time, then drizzle the honey over the pears for the last 30 seconds • Slice the tomatoes • In a bowl, mix the cottage cheese with the zest and juice of ½ a lemon and a pinch of salt and pepper • Slice open the hot ciabatta and load it up with all of your fillings • Dress the salad at the last minute and serve

TAPAS BRUSCHETTA
GOLDEN GRILLED SARDINES

SERVES 4 | 780 CALORIES

Ingredients out • Oven at 400°F • Food processor (fine slicer & metal blade)
• Grill pan, high heat

Bruschetta

2 ciabatta loaves
8 oz cooked beets
balsamic vinegar
1 bunch of fresh basil
1 small bulb fennel
1 lemon
a few sprigs of fresh mint
1 clove garlic
8 ripe cherry or grape tomatoes
4 rashers of prosciutto

Sardines

8 x 3-oz whole sardines,
 scaled and gutted
1 pinch of cayenne pepper

Hummus

1 x 14-oz can of chickpeas
1 heaping tsp smooth peanut butter
1 lemon
1 pinch of cumin seeds
2–3 tbsp fat-free plain yogurt

START COOKING

Trim the edges off the ciabatta lengthways, then cut them in half lengthways and put into the oven to toast, removing when golden • Tip the beets into a shallow bowl, then mash with a potato masher • Drizzle with a little balsamic and season with salt and pepper • Roughly chop half of the basil leaves and toss with the beets

Quarter the fennel bulb, then finely slice it in the processor along with ½ a lemon • Chop the top leafy half off the mint, then add to the bowl, toss together and season to taste • Lightly season the sardines with salt, pepper and the cayenne, then place on the grill to cook for around 3 minutes on each side, or until golden

Swap to the metal blade in the processor • Add the drained chickpeas, peanut butter and the juice of 1 lemon • Rip off and add the remaining basil leaves, cumin seeds and yogurt, then whiz until smooth and season to taste • Rub the toasts with half a garlic clove and the tomatoes, then lay them on a nice serving board with the prosciutto • Squeeze lemon juice over the sardines, then take everything to the table and load up the toasts however you like them

VEGGIE

HAPPY COW BURGERS
OLD-SCHOOL COLESLAW & CORN ON THE COB

Corn
4 corn cobs (husks removed)
1 tsp extra virgin olive oil
1 lime
1 pinch of cayenne pepper

Burgers
1 big bunch of fresh cilantro
1 x 14-oz can of mixed beans
7 oz frozen fava beans
½ tsp cayenne pepper
½ tsp ground cumin
½ tsp ground coriander
1 lemon
1 heaping tbsp all-purpose flour,
  plus extra for dusting
olive oil
2 large ripe tomatoes
1 little gem lettuce or heart of
  romaine
4 gherkins
3 oz feta cheese
4 burger buns
tomato ketchup, to serve

Slaw
½ head of small white and red
  cabbage (roughly 7 oz each)
½ red onion
⅓ cup fat-free plain yogurt
1 heaping tsp grainy mustard

Ingredients out • Kettle boiled • Oven at 250°F • Large lidded saucepan, medium heat • Food processor (metal blade & coarse grater) • Large frying pan, medium-high heat

START COOKING
Put the corn into the saucepan and cover with boiling water and the lid • Put the cilantro stalks into the processor (reserving the leaves), then drain the mixed beans and add, along with the fava beans, a pinch of salt and pepper, the cayenne, cumin, ground coriander, grated lemon zest and flour • Whiz until fine and combined, scraping down the sides of the processor if needed

Tip the mixture onto a generously flour-dusted board, divide into 4 pieces, then roll each piece into a ball and flatten into a patty about 1-inch thick, dusting your hands and the burgers with flour as you go • Pour 2 tablespoons of olive oil into the frying pan, followed by the burgers, pressing them down with a slotted spatula and flipping them when golden • Slice the tomatoes, lettuce and gherkins on a nice serving board and crumble the feta on one side • Put the buns into the oven

Swap to the grater in the processor, then grate the cabbages and peeled red onion, and tip into a bowl • Chop the cilantro leaves and add, with the yogurt, mustard and the juice of the zested lemon, then toss well and season to taste • Drain the corn, place on a platter, drizzle with the extra virgin olive oil and lime juice, and sprinkle with a pinch of salt and the cayenne • Get the buns out of the oven, cut them in half, dollop with ketchup, add the burgers and let everyone build their own

VEGGIE CHILI
CRUNCHY TORTILLA & AVOCADO SALAD

SERVES 4 | 749 CALORIES

Ingredients out • Oven at 400°F • Food processor (metal blade)
• Lidded casserole pan or Dutch oven, high heat • Immersion blender

Chili & rice
1 dried smoked chipotle
   or ancho chile
½ fresh red chile
1 red onion
1 tsp sweet smoked paprika
½ tsp cumin seeds
1–2 garlic cloves
1 big bunch of fresh cilantro
olive oil
2 mixed-color bell peppers
1 x 14-oz can of chickpeas
1 x 14-oz can of black beans
3 ¼ cups passata
1 x 8-oz package of ready-made
   wholegrain brown rice or mixed
   long-grain and wild rice

Salad
4 small soft corn tortillas
2 ripe avocados
¼ cup fat-free plain yogurt, plus
   extra to serve
2 limes
1 head of romaine lettuce
½ English cucumber
1 fresh red chile
1 handful of ripe cherry or grape
   tomatoes

START COOKING

Put the chiles, peeled and halved red onion, paprika and cumin seeds into the processor, squash in the unpeeled garlic through a garlic press, then add the cilantro stalks (reserving the leaves) and 2 tablespoons of oil, and whiz until fine • Tip into the pan, then add the seeded and roughly chopped peppers, drained chickpeas and black beans, a pinch of salt and pepper and the passata, stir well and put the lid on • Fold the tortillas in half, slice into ¼-inch strips, sprinkle onto a baking sheet and pop in the oven until golden and crisp

Put most of the cilantro leaves, a pinch of salt and pepper, half a peeled avocado, the yogurt and the juice from 2 limes into a pitcher and whiz with an immersion blender until silky • Check and adjust the seasoning of the chili, leave the lid off • Remove the tortillas from the oven into a bowl, cut the lettuce into chunky wedges and add to the bowl • Scoop and dot over curls of avocado • Peel the cucumber into ribbons and finely slice half a chile, then scatter both over the top

Make a well in the middle of the chili and tip in the rice, then pop the lid on for the last few minutes to warm the rice through • Pour the dressing over the salad, pick over the remaining cilantro leaves, finely slice the remaining chile and sprinkle over the top along with the halved tomatoes, then toss everything together • Serve with dollops of yogurt

FALAFEL WRAPS
GRILLED VEG & SALSA

SERVES 4 | 602 CALORIES

Ingredients out • Food processor (metal blade) • Large frying pan, medium heat • Grill pan, high heat

Falafel

1 x 14-oz can of mixed beans
1 x 14-oz can of chickpeas
1 lemon
1 tbsp harissa
1 heaping tsp allspice
1 heaping tbsp all-purpose flour
1 bunch of fresh cilantro
olive oil

Sides

2 mixed-color bell peppers
4 scallions
8 small wholewheat tortillas
1 tbsp hot chili sauce
1 cup low-fat cottage cheese
optional: pickled red cabbage

Salsa

1 big handful of heirloom mixed
  ripe tomatoes
½–1 fresh red chile
½ clove garlic
1 lime

START COOKING

Drain the beans and chickpeas and put them into the processor • Finely grate in the lemon zest, then add a pinch of salt and pepper, the harissa, allspice, flour and cilantro stalks (reserving the leaves) • Blitz until smooth, scraping down the sides of the processor if needed • Scrape out the mixture and use clean, wet hands to quickly divide and shape it into 8 patties about ¾-inch thick • Put 1 tablespoon of oil into the frying pan and add the falafels, turning when golden and crisp

Rip the seeds and stalks out of the peppers, tear each one into bite-sized chunks and put on the grill pan with the trimmed and halved scallions and a pinch of salt and pepper, turning when charred • Put the tomatoes, chile and half the cilantro leaves into the processor • Squash in the unpeeled garlic through a garlic press, squeeze in the lime juice, whiz until fine, then season to taste and pour into a serving dish

Pop the tortillas into the microwave on high for 45 seconds or until warm while you swirl the chili sauce into the cottage cheese • Squeeze the juice of half the zested lemon over the charred veggies, then take with the falafels to the table, scattering everything with the rest of the cilantro • Let everyone assemble their own wraps, and serve with pickled red cabbage, if you like

KERALAN VEGGIE CURRY
PAPPADAMS, RICE & MINTY YOGURT

Ingredients out • Kettle boiled • Grill pan, high heat • Medium lidded saucepan, medium heat • Large casserole pan or Dutch oven, low heat • Food processor (metal blade)

Curry

½ head of cauliflower
2 tbsp canola oil
1 heaping tsp black mustard seeds
1 heaping tsp fenugreek seeds
1 heaping tsp turmeric
1 small handful of dried curry leaves
1 thumb-sized piece of gingerroot
2 cloves garlic
6 scallions
1 fresh red chile
1 large bunch of fresh cilantro
2 ripe tomatoes
1 x 14-oz can of light coconut milk
1 x 14-oz can of chickpeas
1 x 8-oz can of pineapple chunks in juice
1 lemon

Rice

1 mug (10 oz) of 10-minute wholegrain brown or basmati rice
10 whole cloves
½ lemon

To serve

4 uncooked pappadams
½ bunch of fresh mint
3 tbsp fat-free plain yogurt
½ lemon

START COOKING

Remove the outer leaves from the cauliflower, then slice it ½-inch thick and put it on the grill pan, turning when lightly charred • Put 1 mug of rice and 2 mugs of boiling water into the medium saucepan with the cloves, lemon half and a pinch of salt, and put the lid on • Pour the oil into the casserole pan, then quickly stir in the mustard and fenugreek seeds, turmeric and curry leaves

Pulse the peeled ginger and garlic, trimmed scallions, chile and cilantro stalks in the processor until fine, then stir into the casserole pan • Roughly chop and add the tomatoes • Pour in the coconut milk, add the drained chickpeas, then tip in the pineapple chunks and their juices • Add the grilled cauliflower, cover, turn the heat up to high and bring to a boil

Put the uncooked pappadams into the microwave on high for a minute or two to puff up • Tear off the top leafy half of the mint and bash to a paste in a pestle and mortar • Stir in the yogurt, add a good squeeze of lemon juice and season with salt and pepper • Squeeze the juice of the remaining lemon into the curry and season to taste • Tear over the cilantro leaves and serve with the rice and pappadams

MODERN GREEK SALAD
SPINACH, CHICKPEA & FETA PARCELS

SERVES 4 | 516 CALORIES

Ingredients out • Oven at 425°F • Food processor (metal blade, thick slicer & fine slicer) • Ovenproof medium frying pan, medium heat • Medium frying pan, medium heat

Parcels

1 x 14-oz can of chickpeas
3 ½ oz feta cheese
2 large handfuls of baby spinach
1 lemon
½ tsp sweet smoked paprika
4 large sheets of phyllo pastry
olive oil

Salad

1 English cucumber
1 small red onion
½ mixed bunch of fresh
    cilantro and mint
1 oz blanched almonds
1 handful of black olives (with pits)
1½ lbs mixed ripe tomatoes
1 head of romaine lettuce
2 tbsp extra virgin olive oil

To serve

fat-free plain yogurt
honey

START COOKING

Drain and add the chickpeas to the processor along with the feta, spinach, lemon zest and paprika, then blitz until combined • Fold a large sheet of phyllo pastry in half, dollop ¼ of the mixture into the center, push your thumb into the middle to make a space for the filling to expand as it cooks, then bring the sides up and very loosely pinch into a parcel • Repeat to make 4 parcels • Add to the ovenproof pan with 1 tablespoon of olive oil and fry for a couple of minutes to crisp up the bottom, then bake in the oven until beautifully golden and crisp

Swap to the thick slicer in the processor • Scratch a fork down the length of the cucumber all the way round, then run it through the processor • Swap to the fine slicer and run through the peeled onion • Tip the veg into a bowl, season with salt, squeeze over the juice of the zested lemon and scrunch to mix • Finely chop and scatter over most of the top leafy half of the cilantro and mint

Put the almonds and olives into the empty frying pan with 1 tablespoon of olive oil • Thickly slice the tomatoes and arrange nicely on a large platter • Slice the lettuce ½-inch thick and add to the platter, then sprinkle over the cucumber and onion, drizzle with the extra virgin olive oil and spoon over the contents from the pan • Serve the parcels with a good dollop of yogurt, a good drizzle of honey and the salad

RICOTTA FRITTERS
TOMATO SAUCE & ZUCCHINI SALAD

SERVES 4 | 408 CALORIES

Ingredients out • *Kettle boiled* • *Large frying pan, medium heat*
• *Large casserole pan or Dutch oven, low heat* • *Food processor (fine grater)*

Sauce

1 oz dried porcini mushrooms
optional: 4 anchovy fillets
1 dried red chile
2 cloves garlic
3 ¼ cups passata
8 black olives (with pits)
½ bunch of fresh basil

Fritters

1 large egg
1½ cups ricotta cheese
1 whole nutmeg, for grating
1 lemon
1½ oz Parmesan cheese
1 heaping tbsp all-purpose flour
olive oil
balsamic vinegar

Salad

14 oz firm green or yellow
   baby zucchini
1 tbsp extra virgin olive oil
1 fresh red chile
½ bunch of fresh mint
1 lemon

START COOKING

Put the porcini into a small bowl and cover with boiling water • Crack the egg into a mixing bowl, add the ricotta, finely grate in ¼ of the nutmeg, the lemon zest and Parmesan, add the flour, then beat together • Put 1 tablespoon of olive oil into the frying pan, then use a tablespoon to spoon in 8 large dollops of the mixture, turning carefully when nice and golden

Put the anchovies (if using) and 1 tablespoon of olive oil into the casserole pan, crumble in the dried chile, and squash in the unpeeled garlic through a garlic press • Finely chop and add the porcini with half their soaking water and the passata, season with salt and pepper and bring to a boil • Squash and add the olives, discarding the pits • Pick and reserve a few basil leaves, then chop the rest and add to the sauce

Grate the zucchini in the processor (you could use a box grater here) and tip into a bowl with a pinch of salt and pepper, the juice of the zested lemon and the extra virgin olive oil • Finely chop and add the chile and the top leafy half of the mint, then toss together • Place the fritters on top of the sauce, then scatter over the reserved basil leaves, drizzle with balsamic and serve with lemon wedges

SWEET & SOUR VEGGIES
SZECHUAN EGGY RICE & CRUNCH SALAD

Ingredients out • *Large frying pan, medium heat* • *Wok, medium heat*
• *Food processor (coarse grater & fine slicer)*

Rice

1 tsp Szechuan pepper
2 x 8-oz packages of ready-made
  wholegrain brown rice
1 lemon
2 tbsp sweet red chili sauce
2 large eggs

Stir-fry

2 mixed-color bell peppers
1 bunch of asparagus (10 oz)
1 fresh red chile
1 thumb-sized piece of gingerroot
2 cloves garlic
Asian sesame oil
4 oz baby corn
1 bunch of fresh cilantro
1 heaping tsp cornstarch
1 x 8-oz can of pineapple chunks
  in juice
1 tbsp honey
2 tbsp sherry vinegar
7 oz beansprouts

Salad

2 carrots
7 oz sugar snap peas
1 bunch of fresh mint
1 lime
reduced-sodium soy sauce

START COOKING

Crumble the Szechuan pepper and rice into the frying pan and squeeze in the lemon juice, tossing regularly • Tear the seeds and stalks out of the peppers and slice into ¾-inch chunks along with the trimmed asparagus • Finely chop the chile, peeled ginger and garlic, then add to the wok with 2 tablespoons of oil • Add the peppers, asparagus and baby corn, tossing regularly

Roughly slice the cilantro stalks and add to the wok (reserving the leaves) • Trim the carrots and coarsely grate in the processor • Swap to the fine slicer and run through the sugar snaps • Tip into a large bowl, rip off and toss through the top leafy half of the mint, then dress with the lime juice and 1 tablespoon of oil, and season to taste with soy sauce

Toss the cornstarch with the veg in the wok, followed by the pineapple and juice, honey, vinegar and beansprouts • Toss well and season to taste with soy sauce • Push the rice to one side of the pan, then pour the chili sauce into the space and let it bubble • Crack in the eggs and stir, gradually pulling in the rice • Serve everything sprinkled with cilantro leaves

CAMEMBERT PARCELS
AUTUMN SALAD & CRANBERRY DIP

Camembert parcels

7 oz Camembert cheese
3 ½ oz raw walnut halves
1 bunch of fresh chives
1 lemon
4 large sheets of phyllo pastry
1 tsp olive oil

Cranberry sauce

2 ½ oz dried cranberries
1 pinch of ground cloves
½ tsp ground ginger
½ cup port wine

Salad

1 pomegranate
2 tbsp balsamic vinegar
2 tbsp extra virgin olive oil
1 red endive
1 green endive
1 eating apple
4 cups watercress

Ingredients out • Food processor (metal blade) • Large frying pan, medium heat • Small saucepan, medium heat • Blender

START COOKING

Tear the Camembert into the processor with the walnuts and half the chives • Finely grate in the lemon zest and blitz until combined • On a clean surface, fold each sheet of phyllo in half widthways • Add ¼ of the mixture across the bottom of one folded sheet in a sausage shape, push your thumb into the center to make a space for the filling to expand as it cooks, and roll it up really loosely, like a long cigar • Repeat until you have 4 parcels • Rub each with olive oil and put into the frying pan, turning until golden and crispy

Put the cranberry sauce ingredients into the small saucepan with a splash of water and leave to bubble away • Halve the pomegranate and squeeze the juice from one half through your fingers onto a large platter • Add the balsamic, extra virgin olive oil, and a pinch of salt and pepper, then finely slice and scatter over the remaining chives • Finely slice the endive bases and break the upper leaves apart • Coarsely grate or matchstick the apple, then add to the platter with the endive and watercress

Blitz the cranberry mixture in the blender until smooth (you may need to add a splash of water) • Pour onto a small platter or into a bowl and serve with the parcels for dipping • Toss the salad at the table, then hold the remaining pomegranate half cut-side down over the salad and bash the back of it with a spoon so the seeds tumble on top

MEXICAN SALAD
CHARRED AVO & POPCORN BEANS

SERVES 4 | 725 CALORIES

Ingredients out • Oven broiler on medium • Medium frying pan, medium heat • Large grill pan, high heat • Blender

Nachos
3 large handfuls of reduced-sodium
   tortilla chips
1 oz Cheddar cheese
1 fresh red chile
1 fresh green chile

Salad
1 x 14-oz can of kidney beans
1 x 14-oz can of mixed beans
olive oil
1 pinch of ground cumin
2 ripe avocados
1 good pinch of ground coriander
4 large handfuls of mixed salad
   leaves

Dressing
2 scallions
1 bunch of fresh cilantro
1 tbsp sliced jalapeños (from a jar)
extra virgin olive oil
2 tbsp fat-free plain yogurt
2 limes

START COOKING

Spread the tortilla chips out in a roasting pan and grate over the Cheddar • Finely slice the chiles, sprinkle all over and pop under the broiler on the middle shelf, removing when golden • Drain all the beans and tip into the frying pan with 1 tablespoon of olive oil and the cumin, tossing regularly until bursting open and crispy

Quarter, pit and peel the avocados, toss with 1 teaspoon of olive oil, salt, pepper and the ground coriander • Place them on the hot grill pan until nicely charred all over, then remove • Trim and halve the scallions, then blitz in the blender with half the cilantro, the jalapeños and a good splash of their vinegar, 1 tablespoon of extra virgin olive oil, the yogurt and the juice of 1 lime, then pour into a bowl

Put the salad leaves into a nice serving bowl with the top leafy half of the remaining cilantro, then arrange the charred avocado in and around the salad and scatter the popcorn beans over the top • Drizzle with 1 teaspoon of extra virgin olive oil, and serve with the cheesy chile tortillas, lime wedges, and the dressing for dunking and drizzling

TASTY DAAL CURRY
WARM TOMATO SALAD & NAAN

SERVES 4 | 696 CALORIES

Ingredients out • Kettle boiled • Oven at 250°F • Food processor (metal blade) • Lidded casserole pan or Dutch oven, high heat • Frying pan, low heat

Daal

1 onion
1 clove garlic
1 thumb-sized piece of gingerroot
1–2 fresh red chiles
1 red bell pepper
1 big bunch of fresh cilantro
canola oil
1 handful of fresh curry leaves
1 tsp turmeric
1 tsp fenugreek seeds
2 tsp mustard seeds
10 oz dried red split lentils
1 x 14-oz can of light coconut milk
4 large handfuls of baby spinach

Salad

1 lb ripe heirloom mixed cherry or
   grape tomatoes
1 lemon
1 tsp chili powder
2 cloves garlic

To serve

2 naan breads, or other flatbreads
fat-free plain yogurt

START COOKING

Put the peeled onion halves, garlic and ginger, the chile, seeded pepper, cilantro stalks and a pinch of salt and pepper into the processor, then blitz until fine • Put 1 tablespoon of oil into the casserole pan with the curry leaves, turmeric, fenugreek seeds and half the mustard seeds, and stir well • Add the blitzed veg and fry for a couple of minutes before adding the lentils, 2 ¾ cups boiling water and the coconut milk • Put the lid on and boil, stirring regularly

Pop the naan breads in the oven • Halve the tomatoes and finely chop half the lemon (rind and all) • Put 1 tablespoon of oil, the chili powder, chopped lemon and remaining mustard seeds into the frying pan • Squash in the unpeeled garlic through a garlic press, squeeze over the remaining lemon juice, add the tomatoes and toss for 30 seconds, then season to taste

Fold the spinach through the daal, remove the naans from the oven, then take everything to the table with a bowl of yogurt • Finish with a scattering of cilantro leaves

SPRING FRITTATA
TOMATO TOASTS, WATERCRESS & PEA SALAD

Ingredients out • Oven broiler on high • Food processor (fine grater & fine slicer) • 10-inch ovenproof frying pan, high heat • Grill pan, high heat

Frittata
2 firm medium green or yellow zucchini
1 bunch of fresh mint
olive oil
8 large eggs
½ tsp truffle oil
1 pinch of cayenne pepper
4 sprigs of fresh thyme
1½ oz pecorino cheese
1 fresh red chile
¾ oz feta cheese

Toasts
4 x ¾-inch slices of ciabatta
1 clove garlic
4 ripe cherry or grape tomatoes
1 tsp dried oregano

Salad
extra virgin olive oil
1 lemon
5 oz fresh peas
4 cups watercress
1 celery heart

START COOKING

Grate the zucchini in the processor, put into a bowl, season well with salt, tear in a few mint leaves, then toss and squeeze to get rid of the excess salty liquid • Put 1 teaspoon of olive oil into the frying pan, sprinkle in the zucchini and fry for a few minutes, stirring often • Beat the eggs in a bowl with the truffle oil, cayenne, thyme leaves and half the finely grated pecorino, then pour the mixture over the zucchini • Stir and mix for a minute, then scatter over the rest of the grated pecorino and put on the top shelf under the broiler until cooked through, fluffy and golden (roughly 5 minutes)

Put the ciabatta slices on the grill pan, turning when golden • Pour 2 tablespoons of extra virgin olive oil onto a serving platter with the lemon juice and a pinch of salt and pepper • Roughly chop the rest of the leafy top half of the mint and scatter over the platter with the peas and watercress • Swap to the fine slicer in the processor, then remove the outer celery stalks (save for another day), slice just the bottom half of the heart and add to the salad with the finely sliced leafy tops

Remove the toasts to a nice serving board, rub each one with the cut side of the garlic and squash in a tomato, then sprinkle with oregano and 1 teaspoon of extra virgin olive oil • Finely slice the chile, then slide the frittata onto the board, scatter with the chile, crumble over the feta and serve with the salad, tossing gently at the last minute

BREAK FAST

SMOKY MAPLE BACON
FLUFFY CORN & CHILE PANCAKES

Pancakes

1 cup self-rising flour
1 large egg
1 cup reduced-fat (2%) milk
1 fresh green chile
1½ oz Cheddar cheese
1 handful of frozen corn
olive oil

Toppings

4 ripe tomatoes
1 ripe avocado
1 lime
½ bunch of fresh cilantro
8 rashers of smoked bacon
  or pancetta
maple syrup
¼ cup fat-free plain yogurt
hot chili sauce

This is an amazing weekend breakfast – it will put a smile on your face, get you going and make you feel really satisfied. A hit of chile wakes you up better than any espresso, trust me.

START COOKING

Whisk the flour, egg and milk in a bowl until smooth • Finely slice the chile, grate the cheese, then fold both into the batter with the corn • Roughly chop the tomatoes and the peeled, pitted avocado, then toss with the juice from ½ a lime, the top leafy half of the cilantro, salt and pepper

Put the bacon or pancetta into a medium frying pan on a medium-low heat, turning when crisp and golden • Drizzle with maple syrup, glaze for 20 seconds, then remove from the heat • Drizzle 1 teaspoon of oil into a small frying pan on a medium heat, add a ladleful of batter and spread it out to the edges • Flip when golden and remove to a plate once done

Place ¼ of the topping and bacon or pancetta on top of the pancake and serve with a dollop of yogurt, a wedge of lime, and chili sauce if you like that extra hit • Repeat with the remaining ingredients and serve as and when they're ready

AVOCADO ON TOAST
FOUR WAYS

AVO & EGG

Fill and boil the kettle • Toast **1 slice of nice bread** • Get a small saucepan on a high heat, fill it with boiling water and add a **pinch of salt** • Swirl the water with a fork, then crack in **1 large super-fresh egg** and poach to your liking • Pit, peel and slice **½ a ripe avocado** • Halve **1 ripe cherry tomato** and rub into the toast, then drizzle with **1 teaspoon of extra virgin olive oil** • Cover with the avocado and scatter with **a few slices of fresh red chile** • Pop your egg on top, bust it open and season to taste

AVO & CRISPY BACON OR PANCETTA

Grill **3 rashers of smoked bacon or pancetta** on a hot grill pan, with **1 slice of nice bread** on the side to soak up the tasty fat • Pit and peel **½ a ripe avocado** • Turn the toast and use a fork to squash the avocado into it, spreading it right to the edges • Add **a little pinch of salt and pepper, a squeeze of lime** or lemon juice, **a few slices of fresh red chile** and **4 fresh basil leaves**, then serve with the crispy bacon or pancetta on top

AVO & SMOKED HAM

Toast **1 slice of nice bread** • Drizzle it with **1 teaspoon of olive oil**, then lay **1 slice of ripe beef tomato** and **1 slice of cooked ham** on top • Pit and peel **½ a ripe avocado** and place on top, then add **a little pinch of salt and pepper** and squeeze **lime** or **lemon juice** into the well with a few drips of oil • Use a vegetable peeler to peel over **½ oz Emmental cheese**, then scatter with **4 fresh basil leaves**

AVO & SMOKED SALMON

Toast **1 slice of nice bread** • Drizzle it with **1 teaspoon of extra virgin olive oil** and cover with **1 oz smoked salmon** • Use a teaspoon to add small bombs of **cream cheese (2 tbsp in total)** on top • Pit **½ a ripe avocado**, then use a teaspoon to curl small nuggets of the flesh over the toast • Finely grate over **a little lemon zest**, then add a squeeze of juice and **a pinch of pepper**

BRING BACK THE TOASTIE (PART 1: HOT SANDWICH HEAVEN)

SERVES 1 | 384 CALORIES

2 fresh chives
2 slices of bread
2 slices of smoked salmon
1 large egg
½ oz Cheddar cheese

SMOKED SALMON & EGG

Chop the chives • Place 1 piece of bread in a sandwich press and drape the smoked salmon in a circle on top, leaving a gap in the middle where you can crack in the egg • Scatter over the chopped chives, finely grate over the Cheddar and season with salt and pepper • Carefully top with the second piece of bread and toast away

SERVES 1 | 310 CALORIES

2 slices of bread
1 ripe tomato
1 oz feta cheese
¼ avocado
2 pinches of dried oregano

GREEK-STYLE

Place 1 piece of bread in a sandwich press, then slice and add the tomato • Crumble over the feta • Peel and roughly chop the avocado, pile on top and scatter with a pinch of oregano • Top with the second piece of bread, scatter with the remaining oregano and toast away

VIVA LA TOASTIE
(PART 2: SOME MORE HOT OPTIONS)

2 slices of bread
1 oz Cheddar cheese
3 button mushrooms
1 small handful of arugula
¼ lemon
½ oz cured chorizo sausage

CLASSIC CHEESE & MUSHROOM

Place 1 piece of bread in a sandwich press, then grate over the cheese • Slice and lay over the mushrooms • Chop the arugula, toss in the lemon juice and pile on top, then top with the second piece of bread • Finely slice the chorizo, lay on the top of the sandwich, clamp down well so they stick together, and toast away

1 oz ricotta cheese
1 heaping tsp honey
½ oz dark chocolate
   (62% cocoa solids, or higher)
1 small banana
2 slices of bread

SWEET NAUGHTY BEGINNING

Beat the ricotta with the honey, smash the chocolate, and peel and roughly chop the banana • Place 1 piece of bread in a sandwich press, then spread the ricotta on top • Lay over the banana and scatter over the chocolate • Top with the second piece of bread and toast away

FANTASTIC GRANOLA
GET UP, GET FED, GET GONE

MAKES 3 × 1 QUART JARS |
332 CALORIES PER PORTION

Granola mix

½ cup whole unsalted raw
   Brazil nuts
¾ cup raw walnut halves
¾ cup unsalted raw pistachios
½ cup unsalted raw pumpkin seeds
¾ cup unsalted raw sunflower seeds
¾ cup raw sesame seeds
4 cups old-fashioned rolled oats
½ cup unsweetened shredded
   coconut
1 tsp ground cinnamon
½ cup dried sour cherries
1 cup soft dried apricots

To serve

maple syrup
milk or fat-free plain yogurt

My suggestion is to buy a big batch of ingredients like the list I've given you here, mix it all up and just grab a handful per person whenever you need it – it will last for months. I love it served with fresh blueberries or pomegranate seeds.

START COOKING

Roughly bash up the nuts and seeds in a pestle and mortar or pulse them in a food processor with a metal blade – I like some fine and some chunky • Mix them with the oats, coconut and cinnamon

Now you've got a choice: you can either mix it with the chopped cherries and apricots and decant it straight into airtight jars to toast as and when you want it, or you can spread it across a couple of large roasting pans and toast it in a preheated oven at 350°F until nicely golden, stirring regularly • Let it cool, then mix in the chopped cherries and apricots and tip into jars to await eating

If you want to toast it as and when you want it, I just put a dry frying pan on a medium heat and add a handful of granola (roughly ⅓ cup) per person • Toast for 3 or so minutes, tossing often to bring out the roasted flavor and crispy texture, until lightly golden and smelling delicious • Stir in a good teaspoon of maple syrup per person and let it get sticky, then serve hot with cold milk or yogurt and fresh seasonal fruit, if you like

SUPERB BOX GRATER
FRUIT SALAD

SERVES 4 | 91 CALORIES

Sesame honey
1 handful of raw sesame seeds
½ small jar of honey

Ripe fruit
1 pear
1 nectarine
1 handful of strawberries
1 banana
1 apple

Dressing
1 orange or lime
a couple of sprigs of fresh mint

To serve
fat-free plain yogurt

This delicious breakfast is simplicity to the hilt, but don't be misled by that. It's beautiful, tasty, and the action of bruising and grating brings out all the natural sugars in the fruit, creating a liquor that gives it shine and juice. Couple that with the warm sesame honey and it's unbelievable. Definitely give it a go.

START COOKING

Toast the sesame seeds in a dry pan, tossing frequently until golden • Mix with the honey, then warm through in the microwave on high for 20 seconds or until warm before using • Keep the rest for another day – it's delicious and lasts a long time

Set up a box grater on a plate, then in long strokes coarsely and carefully grate all the fruit, piece by piece – you can use any slightly firm stone fruit like plums, peaches and nectarines, perfect orchard fruit, strawberries and bananas • Carefully lift off the grater, leaving a lovely pile of grated fruit • Squeeze over the orange or lime juice and drizzle with 2 tablespoons of sesame honey • Roughly chop the mint leaves and sprinkle over, then serve with plain yogurt

FRUIT 'N' NUT COMBOS
SWEETENED COTTAGE CHEESE

SERVES 6 | 189 CALORIES

This is about embracing beautiful combinations of simple ingredients for an instant breakfast. A ¼ cup serving of sweetened cheese per person is more than enough, and if you're not feeding six, the sweetened cheese will keep well in the fridge for a couple of days.

START COOKING

In a bowl, mix **1 tablespoon of honey** and **1 heaping teaspoon of vanilla paste or extract** into **1¼ cups cottage cheese or ricotta** (Greek yogurt is also delicious) • Loosen with a **splash of milk** if needed and whip up, then divide between your plates or bowls • Top with wonderful **fresh fruit** like chopped mango, strawberries and watermelon, **a little squeeze of lime juice** and a scattering of **chopped** or **bashed shelled nuts** like Brazils, almonds or pistachios

SUPER SMOOTHIES
FOUR WAYS TO KICK-START YOUR DAY

You can make all of these smoothies with fresh fruit, but what I like to do is bag up fruit combos and freeze them ahead of when I need them, which eliminates the need to add ice. This will also give you a thicker, even more delicious, cold smoothie that's guaranteed to invigorate and wake you up in the morning.

You can get brilliant frozen fruit from the supermarkets, but with things like bananas, or when there's a glut of seasonal fruit, get into the habit of bagging them up and freezing them yourself. Two minutes of thought one day will save you time every morning for a month, mean you've got treats in the freezer and can even save you money – if you've got fruit that's on the turn and you're not going to eat it, you can freeze it before it goes too far.

GREEN
In a blender, blitz **1 large peeled banana** (ideally pre-chopped and frozen) with **4 large handfuls of baby spinach, 1 cup fresh apple juice** and the **juice from 1 lime**, until smooth

PURPLE
Roughly chop **2 pears (stalks removed)**, put into a blender with **1 cup frozen blueberries** and **⅓ cup fresh apple juice**, then blitz until smooth

ORANGE
Finely grate a **¾-inch piece of peeled gingerroot** into a blender • Peel, trim, roughly chop and add **1 carrot**, and squeeze in the **juice of 1 lime** • Add **1 small frozen chopped mango** and **¾ cup fresh orange juice**, then blitz until smooth

WHITE
In a blender, blitz **1 large peeled banana** (ideally pre-chopped and frozen) with **3 tablespoons of ground almonds, 1 cup reduced-fat (2%) milk** and **1 tablespoon of honey**, until smooth

BEAUTIFUL THINGS HAPPEN WHEN YOU SMILE

ONLY AFTER THE LAST TREE HAS BEEN CUT DOWN,
ONLY AFTER THE LAST RIVER HAS BEEN POISONED,
ONLY AFTER THE LAST FISH HAS BEEN CAUGHT,
ONLY THEN WILL YOU FIND THAT MONEY CANNOT BE EATEN.

A NOTE ON NUTRITION
FROM LAURA PARR – JAMIE'S HEAD NUTRITIONIST

JAMIE AND I HAVE WORKED TOGETHER ON THIS BOOK TO CREATE RECIPES THAT DELIVER TASTY, GOOD-FOR-YOU FOOD, BUT DON'T COMPROMISE ON FLAVOR. THIS ISN'T A DIET BOOK, BUT THE RECIPES HAVE BEEN WRITTEN MINDFULLY TO ACHIEVE A BALANCE BETWEEN CARBOHYDRATES, FRUIT AND/OR VEG, DAIRY AND PROTEIN, WITH THE ODD TREAT RECIPE THROWN IN (THIS IS REAL LIFE AFTER ALL!).

In the US, most foods belong to one of five major food groups (Canada combines the first two):

- fruits
- vegetables
- grain, including bread, cereal, rice, bulgur, quinoa and pasta
- protein, including seafood, lean meat, poultry, eggs, tofu, legumes, nuts and seeds
- dairy, including milk, yogurt and cheese, and alternatives such as calcium-fortified soy milk

It's crucial to strike the right balance between these groups every day. Our typical food choices should include a large variety of fruits and vegetables, as well as whole grains, moderate amounts of lean, protein-rich foods and low-fat dairy products. This is what we've set out to achieve with the majority of these meals – obviously you don't have to have that balance in every single meal you eat, but it is a good guide to aim for on a day-to-day basis.

Eating treats is a part of life, but it's also important to recognize when we're pushing things too far, so we can redress the balance at other meals and get back on track. When we eat and drink, we're putting energy (calories) into our bodies, and understanding the amount of calories we consume is one way of monitoring our food intake in order to try to maintain a healthy weight. We've given you the calorie content per serving of every recipe in this book to encourage

you to start thinking about how each of these meals fits into your daily calorie intake. As a guide, the average moderately active man needs around 2,500 calories a day to maintain a healthy body weight, and the average moderately active woman needs 2,000 calories a day.

By eating a wide range of different foods, you'll stand a greater chance of getting all the nutrients you need. So when you're cooking from this book, just mix up the recipes you choose, picking from all the different chapters. Of course you'll have your favorites, but try to eat a diverse mix – maybe fish a couple of nights a week (go for oily fish like sardines or mackerel once a week), a meat-free recipe on one or two nights, then a variety of beef, pork, lamb or chicken on the rest.

Here are some general tips to help you on your way to a healthier lifestyle. Use these as a rough guide and you'll be heading in the right direction:

- When preparing starchy foods, choose wholegrain options such as wholewheat pasta, brown rice, quinoa or couscous whenever possible.
- Eat lots of fruit and vegetables, as they provide important vitamins and minerals.
- Eat more fish, and aim to have oily fish once a week.
- Cut down on saturated fat and sugar.
- Try to eat less salt – taste your food before seasoning it, as you can always add more salt but you can't take it away. Don't forget a lot of food already has salt in it, so you may not need to add more.
- Drink plenty of water.
- Enjoy your food, but eat less and avoid oversized portions.
- Be as active as possible and aim to maintain a healthy weight.

Above all, enjoy the recipes in this book!

Don't forget, it's vital to balance the amount you eat with your level of activity, as different people have different nutritional requirements, depending on factors such as their age, gender and lifestyle.

No.	KCAL	FAT	SUGAR	SAT FAT
24	795	16.4g	6.2g	6.4g
26	607	19.9g	13.3g	3.7g
28	651	18.4g	17.8g	4.0g
30	557	22.5g	4.4g	3.3g
32	610	19.3g	10.4g	4.5g
34	694	33.3g	17.1g	7.1g
36	625	15.2g	10.1g	5.0g
38	683	19.9g	10.9g	4.3g
40	455	11.1g	12.9g	3.1g
42	607	28.1g	11.5g	9.4g
44	656	23.5g	10.7g	8.5g
46	617	22.0g	16.8g	5.0g
48	666	26.7g	11.1g	8.0g
50	476	15.2g	10.3g	4.7g
52	616	14.3g	12.3g	3.2g
54	738	30.9g	10.5g	6.5g
58	437	14.2g	11.1g	4.8g
60	532	23.8g	16.6g	7.1g
62	625	21.1g	10.9g	5.5g
64	653	23.9g	5.9g	5.2g
66	706	21.1g	9.1g	7.6g
68	585	23.9g	6.4g	5.0g
70	593	13.7g	14.2g	3.6g
72	613	23.8g	7.3g	8.9g
74	556	20.6g	12.3g	5.5g

KCAL 545	FAT 23.8g
SUGAR 3.8g	SAT FAT 5.5g

76

KCAL 576	FAT 19.4g
SUGAR 7.8g	SAT FAT 6.7g

78

KCAL 558	FAT 19.4g
SUGAR 11.5g	SAT FAT 6.3g

80

KCAL 663	FAT 25.2g
SUGAR 11.0g	SAT FAT 7.4g

82

KCAL 614	FAT 24.8g
SUGAR 11.9g	SAT FAT 7.2g

84

KCAL 582	FAT 22.4g
SUGAR 8.8g	SAT FAT 6.3g

88

KCAL 611	FAT 22.9g
SUGAR 22.4g	SAT FAT 5.7g

90

KCAL 582	FAT 28.6g
SUGAR 7.5g	SAT FAT 7.2g

92

KCAL 685	FAT 21.7g
SUGAR 16.8g	SAT FAT 4.8g

94

KCAL 641	FAT 23.2g
SUGAR 14.6g	SAT FAT 5.4g

96

KCAL 574	FAT 19.4g
SUGAR 3.7g	SAT FAT 6.2g

98

KCAL 632	FAT 13.9g
SUGAR 8.4g	SAT FAT 5.4g

102

KCAL 687	FAT 25.0g
SUGAR 14.2g	SAT FAT 7.4g

104

KCAL 650	FAT 21.9g
SUGAR 13.5g	SAT FAT 8.0g

106

KCAL 587	FAT 16.9g
SUGAR 13.8g	SAT FAT 7.3g

108

KCAL 523	FAT 22.2g
SUGAR 10.1g	SAT FAT 6.6g

110

KCAL 538	FAT 21.5g
SUGAR 8.5g	SAT FAT 9.9g

112

KCAL 525	FAT 29.0g
SUGAR 13.1g	SAT FAT 8.1g

114

KCAL 629	FAT 16.4g
SUGAR 4.6g	SAT FAT 6.4g

118

KCAL 396	FAT 13.1g
SUGAR 15.1g	SAT FAT 3.7g

120

KCAL 457	FAT 13.4g
SUGAR 6.4g	SAT FAT 1.7g

122

KCAL 458	FAT 11.6g
SUGAR 5.3g	SAT FAT 1.3g

124

KCAL 559	FAT 19.5g
SUGAR 8.8g	SAT FAT 3.4g

126

KCAL 525	FAT 19.6g
SUGAR 16.6g	SAT FAT 3.6g

128

KCAL 407	FAT 21.0g
SUGAR 17.0g	SAT FAT 4.2g

130

KCAL 491 / **FAT** 20.9g / **SUGAR** 8.5g / **SAT FAT** 4.5g — 132	**KCAL** 489 / **FAT** 11.8g / **SUGAR** 8.3g / **SAT FAT** 1.7g — 134	**KCAL** 611 / **FAT** 21.5g / **SUGAR** 15.6g / **SAT FAT** 2.1g — 136	**KCAL** 603 / **FAT** 17.9g / **SUGAR** 6.5g / **SAT FAT** 7.0g — 138	**KCAL** 569 / **FAT** 32.7g / **SUGAR** 7.3g / **SAT FAT** 7.7g — 140
KCAL 549 / **FAT** 18.8g / **SUGAR** 15.7g / **SAT FAT** 2.7g — 142	**KCAL** 441 / **FAT** 19.1g / **SUGAR** 7.9g / **SAT FAT** 5.6g — 144	**KCAL** 474 / **FAT** 14.2g / **SUGAR** 7.6g / **SAT FAT** 2.9g — 146	**KCAL** 431 / **FAT** 11.7g / **SUGAR** 13.7g / **SAT FAT** 1.8g — 148	**KCAL** 633 / **FAT** 20.8g / **SUGAR** 14.3g / **SAT FAT** 5.9g — 150
KCAL 452 / **FAT** 17.9g / **SUGAR** 8.6g / **SAT FAT** 5.6g — 152	**KCAL** 516 / **FAT** 17.3g / **SUGAR** 9.9g / **SAT FAT** 2.2g — 154	**KCAL** 648 / **FAT** 22.4g / **SUGAR** 4.2g / **SAT FAT** 7.8g — 156	**KCAL** 565 / **FAT** 22.8g / **SUGAR** 14.1g / **SAT FAT** 3.2g — 158	**KCAL** 446 / **FAT** 8.8g / **SUGAR** 11.4g / **SAT FAT** 1.5g — 160
KCAL 680 / **FAT** 26.2g / **SUGAR** 17.2g / **SAT FAT** 4.3g — 162	**KCAL** 399 / **FAT** 20.7g / **SUGAR** 12.0g / **SAT FAT** 5.5g — 164	**KCAL** 634 / **FAT** 22.8g / **SUGAR** 10.1g / **SAT FAT** 6.7g — 166	**KCAL** 504 / **FAT** 21.3g / **SUGAR** 7.8g / **SAT FAT** 2.3g — 168	**KCAL** 581 / **FAT** 27.3g / **SUGAR** 5.4g / **SAT FAT** 5.4g — 172
KCAL 673 / **FAT** 18.1g / **SUGAR** 8.7g / **SAT FAT** 3.0g — 174	**KCAL** 622 / **FAT** 21.5g / **SUGAR** 16.4g / **SAT FAT** 6.6g — 176	**KCAL** 603 / **FAT** 26.4g / **SUGAR** 9.5g / **SAT FAT** 8.3g — 178	**KCAL** 635 / **FAT** 17.7g / **SUGAR** 15.8g / **SAT FAT** 4.6g — 180	**KCAL** 553 / **FAT** 20.4g / **SUGAR** 7.3g / **SAT FAT** 4.0g — 182

KCAL 526	FAT 29.6g
SUGAR 13.8g	SAT FAT 7.5g

184

KCAL 613	FAT 23.7g
SUGAR 8.6g	SAT FAT 6.2g

186

KCAL 687	FAT 20.9g
SUGAR 16.5g	SAT FAT 6.0g

188

KCAL 620	FAT 18.4g
SUGAR 17.6g	SAT FAT 3.8g

190

KCAL 644	FAT 29.2g
SUGAR 10.6g	SAT FAT 5.7g

192

KCAL 562	FAT 12.7g
SUGAR 5.6g	SAT FAT 3.2g

194

KCAL 586	FAT 24.0g
SUGAR 5.0g	SAT FAT 8.9g

196

KCAL 651	FAT 25.0g
SUGAR 6.9g	SAT FAT 5.5g

198

KCAL 649	FAT 23.2g
SUGAR 4.3g	SAT FAT 4.8g

200

KCAL 642	FAT 28.4g
SUGAR 23.8g	SAT FAT 7.4g

204

KCAL 608	FAT 24.9g
SUGAR 9.2g	SAT FAT 5.2g

206

KCAL 405	FAT 16.8g
SUGAR 9.3g	SAT FAT 4.5g

208

KCAL 484	FAT 18.2g
SUGAR 12.6g	SAT FAT 5.1g

210

KCAL 638	FAT 21.7g
SUGAR 8.1g	SAT FAT 5.7g

212

KCAL 665	FAT 17.8g
SUGAR 14.4g	SAT FAT 5.4g

214

KCAL 491	FAT 21.5g
SUGAR 14.4g	SAT FAT 6.2g

216

KCAL 780	FAT 27.5g
SUGAR 10.0g	SAT FAT 6.6g

218

KCAL 619	FAT 18.8g
SUGAR 18.3g	SAT FAT 4.6g

222

KCAL 749	FAT 25.2g
SUGAR 16.7g	SAT FAT 4.8g

224

KCAL 602	FAT 15.5g
SUGAR 9.9g	SAT FAT 4.7g

226

KCAL 725	FAT 24.4g
SUGAR 11.7g	SAT FAT 6.7g

228

KCAL 516	FAT 22.0g
SUGAR 17.5g	SAT FAT 5.9g

230

KCAL 408	FAT 27.7g
SUGAR 10.0g	SAT FAT 11.2g

232

KCAL 481	FAT 18.6g
SUGAR 22.6g	SAT FAT 3.4g

234

KCAL 651	FAT 37.3g
SUGAR 23.3g	SAT FAT 9.9g

236

KCAL 725	FAT 35.4g
SUGAR 4.7g	SAT FAT 7.6g

238

KCAL 696	FAT 23.2g
SUGAR 14.1g	SAT FAT 6.9g

240

KCAL 468	FAT 28.8g
SUGAR 8.6g	SAT FAT 5.4g

242

KCAL 477	FAT 17.0g
SUGAR 11.7g	SAT FAT 6.1g

246

KCAL 269	FAT 17.9g
SUGAR 2.2g	SAT FAT 3.9g

248

KCAL 268	FAT 18.7g
SUGAR 2.1g	SAT FAT 4.7g

248

KCAL 256	FAT 15.3g
SUGAR 2.4g	SAT FAT 4.3g

248

KCAL 303	FAT 19.5g
SUGAR 2.8g	SAT FAT 5.1g

248

KCAL 384	FAT 16.6g
SUGAR 1.8g	SAT FAT 5.3g

250

KCAL 310	FAT 11.9g
SUGAR 4.8g	SAT FAT 5.4g

250

KCAL 372	FAT 17.8g
SUGAR 2.2g	SAT FAT 8.6g

252

KCAL 387	FAT 12.5g
SUGAR 33.7g	SAT FAT 7.2g

252

KCAL 332	FAT 17.2g
SUGAR 16.1g	SAT FAT 4.2g

254

KCAL 91	FAT 0.6g
SUGAR 17.5g	SAT FAT 0.1g

256

KCAL 189	FAT 9.4g
SUGAR 12.9g	SAT FAT 1.9g

258

KCAL 146	FAT 1.1g
SUGAR 26.2g	SAT FAT 0.2g

260

KCAL 100	FAT 0.4g
SUGAR 18.3g	SAT FAT 0.0g

260

KCAL 113	FAT 0.5g
SUGAR 20.8g	SAT FAT 0.1g

260

KCAL 340	FAT 19.0g
SUGAR 24.8g	SAT FAT 2.7g

260

Thank you

I want to start by saying a few important thanks to some dear friends who I work with on a regular basis. Most of the people I've chosen to work with on these books have been working with me for a long, long time, although of course there are always a few young whippersnappers coming into the fold! We're a close-knit unit, and whether I'm talking about the talented teams that support me in creating these books, the fantastic personal team that organizes my life or the dedicated TV crews that make my shows – everything we work on together takes hard work, enthusiasm and energy, which you guys never fail to deliver. So my heartfelt thanks go as follows:

To my dear family, including Gennaro of course, for your continued love and support, thank you.

To David, or Lord Admiral, Loftus – what amazing pictures, brother. As usual you've excelled yourself – lots of love.

TALENTED GANG

Huge thanks and love to my incredible food team: a wonderful mob of brilliant, talented, massively hard-working cooks, chefs, food stylists, editors and nutritionists. You all make sure everything I dream up actually happens, and your uncompromised commitment to making sure we have the best, most reliable cookbooks is never taken for granted. To the foodies and stylists: mother hen Ginny Rolfe and Sarah "Tiddles" Tildesley – thank you so much for everything. To my Greek sister Georgie Socratous, bless you and thank you. Christina "Boochie" Mackenzie, thanks for reining in my swearing, Phillippa Spence, brilliant job pink cheeks, my gorgeous graduate Jodene Jordan, my Brazilian banana Almir Santos and sweet, hard-working Amy Cox – thank you guys. Shout out as well to Barnaby Purdy for his creative energy and Becky Bax for all the help on the shoots. Big love to Abigail "Scottish" Fawcett for all your brilliant help with recipe testing.

To my cracking food teamers back at the office: Pete Begg ♪ they call it, they call it, they call it, they call it … AP ♪ and gorgeous ladies Claire Postans, Jo Lord, Helen Martin and Bobby Sebire. You give me amazing support and keep our team on track; I couldn't do it without you. Huge thanks to my nutrition ninjas, who worked closely with me across every recipe in this book: Laura "**** ninja" Parr and Mary Lynch – great job girls.

To my wonderful girls on words: Rebecca "Rubs" Walker, my NEW editor, thanks for doing an absolutely brilliant job. Thanks as well to the rest of my editorial team, curly/straight-haired Bethan O'Connor and Malou Herkes. And of course, to Katie Bosher, my EX-editor – thanks for everything as usual. You started this journey with us in London, and helped us finish it from the other side of the world.

BLESS YOUR HEARTS

Thanks and love to my lovely publishers at Penguin, who have been just perfect for the last 15 years. You trust me and believe in my instincts, which is amazing. To Tom Weldon, my good friend and the big boss at Penguin, thank you for all your support. To Penguin's brilliant creative director John Hamilton, thank you for all your guidance throughout the books and over the years – still loving it, mate. Thank you to Louise Moore and Lindsey Evans. To the wonderful women on production, Juliette Butler and Janis Barbi – the level of stress and standards you work to are amazing, big big thanks. And to the rest of the cracking team: Tamsin English, Claire Purcell, Jo Wickham, Clare Pollock, Elizabeth Smith, Chantal Noel, Kate Burton, Lucy Beresford-Knox, Nathan Hull, Naomi Fidler, Stuart Anderson and Anna Derkacz – thank you. And finally, to Nick Lowndes and his team of lovely copy-editors, proofreaders and indexers: Annie Lee, Caroline Pretty,

Pat Rush, Shauna Bartlett and Caroline Wilding. Thank you for being so fantastic, diligent, caring, brilliant, clever people, for putting up with my obsessive tweaks, changes and bending of the rules when it comes to the English language, and thank you for working so tightly with my words girls – what a team we have together.

Massive thanks to the lovely girls and guys at Interstate, Jayne Connell, Lucy Self, Christina Beani, Louise Draper, Nigel Gray, Iain Hutchinson, Brian Simpson and Ben Watts. It's always a pleasure working with you, and as per usual I love the beautiful, clean, fresh designs – thanks for helping me make this so good (interstateteam.com).

Thanks also to the gang at Superfantastic, Simon Collins, James Verity and Rachael Ball Risk, who did the cover – great job. It's always fun working with you guys (wearesuperfantastic.com).

Big shout out to my CEO John Jackson, managing director Tara Donovan and my deputy/the matrix/ the black widow/the Theydon tongue Louise Holland for all their amazing support. Big thanks to my personal team: Richard Herd, Holly Adams, Amelia Crook, Sy Brighton, Beth Powell and Paul Rutherford. You guys arrange the chaos that is my life and, most importantly, make sure that I have the right amount of time with my family, as well as unadulterated time to concentrate on my books and everything that surrounds them. Thanks as well to Therese McDermott, my PR manager Peter Berry and the lovely Louisa James on marketing for all their help. And to the rest of the guys at my offices, thanks so much for all the hard work you put in daily on my behalf.

Close-knit unit

And now to the gang at Fresh One Productions . . . half of you lot have been with me a very long time and the other half are freelancers, but all of you are incredibly talented and devoted to whatever project I throw you on. First and foremost, a massive thank you to Zoe Collins, Roy Ackerman and Jo Ralling, who are the heart of Fresh One and genuinely brilliant, talented people. We've built Fresh One together and it's a truly brilliant British independent production company with heart, soul and massively high standards and I'm so proud. Thank you to Nicola Pointer, Mike Matthews and Emily Taylor, the most wonderful, talented series producer, series director and production manager for all their support. To keep up with me and do what you do at the level you do is phenomenal – I really appreciate it and the long hours. Thanks as well to the rest of the brilliant production team: Nicola Georgiou, Gudren Claire, Katie Millard, Nicola Hartley, Shuo Huang, Kathryn Inns, Kirsten Hemingway, Dee Driscoll and Joseph Spiteri-Paris.

WONDERFUL MOB

To Luke Cardiff, an amazing cameraman, and gaffer Mike Sarah – you guys have been with me since day one on *The Naked Chef* and I really appreciate every single job I do with you. And to the rest of the fantastic crew and camera team who are super, super talented and top boys, Dave Miller, Jonathan Dennis the jib, Simon Weekes, focus pullers Pete Bateson and Mihalis Margaritis, grip Andy Young, Crispin Larratt and Godfrey Kirby on sound, Paul Casey, Matt Cardiff, Sean Webb, Louise Harris, Steffen Vala and Joe "son of Mike" Gavshon-Sarah. Shout out to the Timeslice team and their massive camera rig. Big thanks as well to the hard-working edit team: Jen Cockburn, Tony Graynoth, Dan James, Dan Goldthorp, Steve Flatt, Barbara Graham, Joanna Roscoe and James Hart.

LOVING IT

This book has been massively connected with the accompanying TV series so huge thanks to the head of Channel 4, Jay Hunt, and to their daytime commissioner, David Sayer, for being brilliant, trusting me and letting me get on with it. Thanks to Tim and Sarah Mead and their gang, and Emma Evison, John Artley and the rest of their team for the integration support.

Thank you to Maria Comparetto who keeps me looking presentable on these shoots, and to lovely Julie Akeroyd and Lima O'Donnell. Big shout out of course to the three Gavins and Frank who kept the crew beautifully fed and did an unbelievable job (mobilemouthful.com). And thank you to Zoot & Steve for all your help.

NICE ONE GUYS

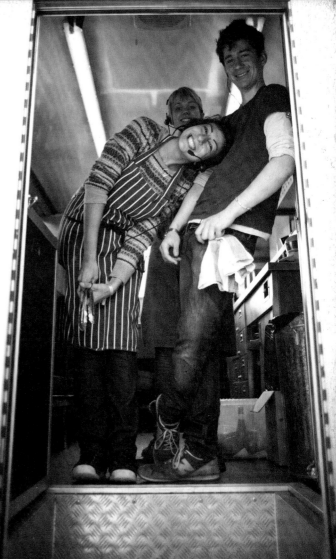

INDEX

Recipes marked v are suitable for vegetarians